MW01657338

THE POWER OF REAL ESTATE

A step by step guide to building generational wealth through homeownership

ANTHONY C. BAILEY

CONTENTS

INTRODUCTION

The American Dream: owning a home. What is owning a home? Self Pride? Accomplishment? Legacy? All of the above. In addition, homeownership is a tool utilized to build generational wealth. Real estate has been used to build wealth through the equity gained over time. This is used as leverage to invest in education, business, or other real estate. If you've played Monopoly, nothing could be farther from the truth, buy a piece of property, leverage the equity, buy more real estate...buy the block.

Before you buy the block, what does it take to be a homeowner? Let's start with one piece of property. Once you understand what it takes to be a homeowner, obtaining, maintaining, and sustaining the home allows you to build generational wealth. I'll be honest, getting a home can be daunting and filled with anxiety, but with the correct information and tools, you'll be a homeowner before you know it.

This book is to be used as a guide to building generational wealth through homeownership. As you go through this, it is recommended to go through it in full once and then come back to it as a reference guide. This is a multipurpose book. It can be a guide, workbook, reference book, manual, etc. It is for you to choose what best works for you; however you choose, use it. Use this to speak with peers and/or partners to discuss what options may work. Create discussion groups with individuals that have gone through real estate investing to verify some of the strategies that are mentioned. The point is to use it to your advantage.

As an investor, I have failed and gained. We discuss what to look for to avoid significant loss. With patience, there is great reward. With knowledge, this is power. With a growth mindset, there is an abundance of wealth. Although we focus on financial wealth, to be able to be financially wealthy, one needs to have a healthy mindset. We start this manuscript with the intention of teaching the mindset one needs to obtain in order to decipher and process the information that follows.

The intention is to build generational wealth both mentally and financially.

- Anthony C. Bailey

MODULE 1: **MINDSET**

1.1 Mindset

You would be surprised at how much the mind is capable of. Most individuals need more self-confidence and effort to recognize their abilities. They are oblivious to their mental dominance. The vast majority of individuals are unaware that they have the power to influence their thoughts and alter their lives for better outcomes and material success.

To harness what the mind possesses, one needs to acknowledge its power and focus on having a growth mindset. A growth mindset allows one to manifest their life in a positive direction. They think, speak, and act in ways that place them in situations that offer positive outcomes.

1.2 Fixed Mindset and Growth Mindset

Those with a fixed mindset consider intelligence a fixed trait rather than a collection of skills that may be developed over time.

With a growth mindset, on the other hand, even one's most fundamental skills may be cultivated through consistent effort and practice; natural intelligence and ability are only the foundations on which one can build. In other words, practice does make perfect. If you think about it, you can achieve it. Just because you don't know doesn't mean you won't. Get the point?

Carol Dweck, a psychologist, coined the words "growth mindset" and "fixed mindset" in her book "Mindset: The New Psychology of Achievement." These perspectives represent two different ways of thinking about IQ, skills, and character traits.

Some people have a "fixed mindset," which is the conviction that their IQ and skill levels are unchangeable. Individuals with a "fixed mindset" consider their abilities and traits static, something they were either born with or not. Hence, they avoid situations that may reveal their limits and frequently dread failure for fear of further reinforcing such beliefs.

Conversely, those who adopt a growth mindset believe that their innate intellect and skill set can be enhanced through practice, perseverance, and applying previously acquired knowledge. Those with a growth mindset welcome difficulties as learning experiences and aren't scared to experiment despite the risk of making mistakes. People believe they can improve their skills and abilities with time and hard work.

What differentiates those with a growth mindset from those with a fixed mindset is how they deal with adversity and failure. Those with a fixed mindset see setbacks as proof of incompetence. Those who adopt a growth mindset, on the other hand, see setbacks as opportunities to grow and develop. They understand that setbacks are not fatal but a necessary part of the road to success.

Moreover, those with a growth mindset are more willing to accept difficulties and try new things. They think that by pushing themselves outside of their comfort zone, they will be able to learn new things and enhance their talents. In contrast, those with a fixed mindset tend to shy away from new experiences for fear of failing because they believe they lack the requisite skills. You will fail sometimes; those are the learning experiences.

The influence of one's thinking extends well beyond one's own opinions and outlook. It affects how people pursue their ambitions, engage in their professions, and interact with others around them. A growth mindset encourages a person to strive for great things. They can bounce back quickly from failure and keep going even when times get tough. They are open to criticism and see it as a way to grow, so they are more inclined to seek input.

In contrast, people with a fixed mindset tend to set conservative goals. They may not fully pursue them because they fear failure or rejection. They may also struggle with receiving feedback or criticism, as it challenges their self-image and can be perceived as a personal attack.

It is important to note that mindset is not a fixed trait but a continuum that can be developed and nurtured over time. By recognizing the power of a growth mindset, individuals can intentionally cultivate it in themselves and others. This can be achieved through various methods, such as reframing failures as learning opportunities, embracing challenges, seeking feedback, and adopting a continuous improvement mindset.

The attitude of a Fixed Mindset

Such people think that someone who is naturally gifted artistically doesn't need to put in any effort to produce quality work.

They think success is the result of innate ability rather than hard work.

There is a higher probability of cheating on exams for these people. They act this way because they are self-conscious about being seen as intellectual lightweights (which is what they believe). They don't try to prepare for exams or quizzes since they don't think it will help them do better.

A person with a fixed mindset thinks one must be naturally gifted with arithmetic to figure out how to solve it. If you figure it out the first time, you need to be more clever to do it right the second time.

Individuals with a fixed mindset think there are only three possible levels of brain intelligence: brilliant, ordinary, and stupid. They think there's nothing one can do to improve mental faculties.

The attitude of a Growth Mindset

If you need help understanding how to solve a math issue the first time, a person with a growth mindset thinks you can improve with time, practice, and effort.

Individuals with a growth mindset are highly motivated to acquire knowledge and skills and persist in the face of challenges. In the words of Winston Churchill, a former Prime Minister of Great Britain during World War II, they embodied the spirit of "never, ever, ever giving up".

They put in extra effort because they know they can do better if they try. As far as they're concerned, a lack of success in any given endeavor indicates that they must put in more effort in the future.

Robert Sternberg, author of "Successful Intelligence," says, "It is apparent that experience, training, and personal effort lead people the rest of the way," even though "people may start with differing [abilities]."

Power of Brain Training

Using your head and honing your reasoning abilities are crucial to your daily routine. Your brain is a muscle, if you make it a practice to challenge your brain with games and puzzles, it improves your cognitive skills and helps you deal with challenges in and out of the classroom.

The cells in your brain are known as neurons. Neurons use electricity for information transmission and retrieval (yes, small electrical pulses exist in your body).

Your brain constantly generates new neurons.

This new neural connectivity, however, will not survive without activity.

Those with a growth mindset can maximize the benefits of these newly formed connections between brain cells. They never stop growing intellectually and emotionally, gaining wisdom and insight with time.

A characteristic of a growth mindset is perseverance in the face of setbacks and a willingness to push oneself even when results are disappointing. When faced with adversity, the growth mindset helps one persevere and even prosper.

Think about it for a moment, what kind of mindset do you have—a fixed or a growth one?

If you said "fixed mindset," let's rewind before you made that decision. Having a "growth mindset" as a newborn is perfectly normal. Educating yourself starts the moment you are born. The list of things you've mastered includes sitting up, crawling, walking, talking, using a straw for drinking, walking, feeding yourself, and so on. You persisted despite the challenges you faced. You eventually succeeded because you kept practicing and honing your skills (a trait indicative of a growth mindset).

The key is to remember that at times of great challenge, your brain is developing rapidly. The key is to never, ever, ever give up!

1.3 Change your words, Change your Mindset

Things you say matter. The words you utter go into existence. Understand that when you are speaking, the words manifest into reality. The difference in mindsets can be seen in these examples:

Growth Mindset

As far as knowledge goes, the sky's the limit for me.
Even when I'm angry, I keep working.
I need to test my limits.

Each time I make a mistake, I grow as a person.
Give me some credit where credit is due.
I will be motivated if you achieve.

Fixed Mindset

Either I have a talent for it, or I don't.
When I become mad, I give up.
When questioned, I tend to shut down.

I'm only helpful if I succeed.
Say something nice about my intelligence.
In case you succeed, it will make me feel unsafe.

Growth vs. Fixed Mindset Perspective

Your mindset can make all the difference in your pursuit of success and personal development. Consider these opposing perspectives and their impact on your approach to challenges and opportunities:

Opportunity vs. Threat
Invite vs. Avoid
Learn vs. Hide
Challenge vs. Problem

Improve vs. Useless
Work vs. Deny
Crave vs. Defend

1.4 Five Steps Formula To Get On a New Level

1. Change your beliefs
2. Do what the new you do
3. Believe in Yourself: Achieving the Impossible
4. Your interpersonal game
5. Connect with your inner baby

1. **Change your beliefs:**

Who You are

To reach the next level, you need more than just talent. You have to make up a whole new self-image. You need to develop a vision of your life and where you want to be. In this context, the word "vision" refers to a mental image of one's ultimate goals in life. You may think of this as defining what constitutes success in your professional, personal, or interpersonal life.

What is it that is blocking your sight?

Having a goal in mind is crucial to figuring out what you need in terms of personal growth and then doing something about it.

It would help if you now had a comprehensive understanding of what constitutes success across all areas of your life and which factors are most important to you. In a nutshell, that's what you're picturing. Vision may be compared to the image on the jigsaw puzzle box. It helps you stay on track and see the big picture of your objectives.

In other words, your vision should provide a comprehensive picture of your desired future state, including the kind of life you see, how you imagine living, and the accomplishments you want to attain. The level of detail, however, is optional.

Who you aren't

If you could achieve anything, what would it be? How many of those have you made an effort to accomplish or acquire? What have you avoided doing because you believed you couldn't succeed due to factors inside and beyond your control, such as your gender, nationality, family background, and more? If you put these assumptions to the test, you'll discover that you're far more robust and competent than you give yourself credit for.

2. **Do what the new you do**

Step into the role now that you have a clearer idea of who you are. With this new you, what would you do? What kind of demeanor do you have? Your thoughts? How does this new you behave? What used to be OK has changed. Transform into this new person, and your behavior and outcomes will naturally follow suit. Make your choices and your life reflect your conclusions.

3. **Believe in Yourself: Achieving the Impossible**

To have faith is to see what one doubts or disbelieves as valid and feasible. Do you like the person you are? What percentage of your dreams do you believe you can achieve? To help you see it, consider your proudest accomplishment.

Only some people believed you could pull it off. You may have even had someone tell you or urge you to stop. When you had to rely only on yourself for motivation, you must have found it within yourself to muster the fortitude necessary to get the job done. All of this demonstrates that it is possible to get such results. This is proof positive that you are capable of having faith.

4. **Your interpersonal game**

As you listen, you take in not just the words but also the feelings and emotions conveyed by those words and the person speaking them. Feelings are universal, and so is empathy. Remember that nonverbal cues are far more significant in communication than words. Listen intently to the context of what others are saying. Feelings may be conveyed via nonverbal gestures. Strive to put yourself in the shoes of the person you're talking to. More than just studying how to communicate effectively is required. The only way to resolve a problem is with a comprehensive set of tools; even those only get you so far.

You will have less than half (or even 25%) of the needed information. You can only give it your all once you have that one thing. None of the world's excellent dispute resolution, negotiating, and interpersonal communication abilities can help you much.

5. **Connect with your inner baby**

Learning new methods and techniques is essential for dealing effectively with change and meeting new difficulties. This is what normal and content infants do over and over again. Maintaining a connection with one's "inner baby" propensity for learning is essential for success for adults and children as they develop.

I am an inquisitive person,
Because I keep tumbling.

Now that it's done, I can only chuckle.
I try out several various phrases and utterances.

I'm never, ever going to
give up learning to walk.
Connect yourself to your inner baby.

I'll try anything.
I'd like to meet everyone!
I LOVE a challenge!

Who, when their fundamental requirements are met, are the happiest individuals on Earth by nature? The young ones! Imagine a one-year-old learning to build blocks and then being frustrated as they fall over, or children who are just learning to walk and are overjoyed to be standing up and on the verge of independence. For children, the satisfaction of finally cracking a complex problem is a significant source of happiness. They still need to be made aware of the significance of both success and failure, as they haven't developed a sensitivity to the opinions of others.

1.5 Principles of a Winning Mindset

- **Find your purpose.**

When you have a clear sense of why you're here, you can go forward confidently and resolved, ready to implement your plan.

- **Take care of your mind.**

Every day, people are attacked by a barrage of anxious thoughts that leave them hopeless and disoriented. To succeed, you must learn to take care of your mind and steer it back into being focused and powerful.

- **Clear out the noise.**

The more you let doubtful thoughts into your head, the less likely you are to be able to keep yourself focused long enough to do what you set out to do.

- **Embrace failure.**

If you fail at anything, see it as a chance to improve your knowledge and skills before trying again.

- **Never give up.**

Developing a victorious frame of mind is an ongoing endeavor that calls for undivided attention and concentration on your part.

1.6 Creating a Wealthy Mindset

Now that you have a growth mindset let's turn that into a wealthy mindset. Having a positive attitude about money and the ability to bring it into your life requires a commitment to lifelong learning and the pursuit of new intellectual challenges. How you approach problems and evaluate possibilities allows you to find stability in your life and pave the way to financial success and a good standard of living.

The meaning of "empowerment attitude" varies from person to person, but it typically involves a strong will to succeed financially. You need to formulate a strategy and see it through. Find out how much of your capital you can affordably invest in a particular field before you go bankrupt. It's essential to adjust your strategy when your bankroll fluctuates.

You will spend much time trying until your outlook, assumptions, beliefs, and abilities to earn riches are all in good shape.

If you want to be financially secure enough to set your hours, take care of your family, and work on causes that matter to you, you must learn how to create wealth and keep it safe.

Learn to think like a wealthy person by giving yourself the tools you need to succeed: educate yourself on the topic, set your goal, build your network, learn financial planning, etc. What follows are strategies that have been used successfully by the rich repeatedly and are proven to bring about financial independence.

- Refrain from getting into debt by spending more money than you have. Spend money on necessities and put the remainder into savings or investments. Investments need to be made with caution and forethought. Take steps to ensure that your money is making money.
- Trust the universe and the power of attraction. The best way to change your mindset regarding money is to focus on it, imagine yourself affluent, and discard any limiting beliefs you may have.
- The key to financial success is debt elimination. It would help if you hurried to finish paying off your debt.
- Invest in real estate assets to increase your wealth. Acquire funding-capable assets.
- If you spend more than you make and don't put any of your cash into investments that can increase your wealth, you will ultimately run out of money. To guarantee that one's retirement savings increase at a rate greater than inflation, one must continue to invest throughout retirement.

Here are some guidelines that might be the basis for your strategy:

1. **Set goals**

When first starting, it is optional to grasp the whole picture. Avoid complexity by keeping things simple. Make plans for the next 12 months. What goals would you want to see realized throughout the next 12 months?

Set specific and realistic goals for what you want to achieve during the first year of your wealth-building journey. This could include starting a side business, saving a certain amount of money, or investing in stocks or real estate. Break down your goals into smaller, actionable steps that you can take daily or weekly.

By focusing on short-term goals and taking action consistently, you'll start to see progress toward your larger wealth-building goals. As you gain more experience and knowledge, you can adjust your plans and set new goals for the future. Remember that building wealth is a long-term process, and staying patient, persistent, and focused on your goals is important.

2. **Decide on strategies**

If you want to succeed in reaching your objectives, you'll need to settle on a plan of action. Success requires you to put effort into developing yourself. Attending courses and learning new methods will be beneficial for you. Integrate your unique insights into your strategy.

No two people have the exact same experiences or perspectives, and by incorporating your unique strengths and knowledge, you can create a plan of action that is tailored to your specific goals and circumstances. Continuously refining your approach based on your own experiences and insights can help you stay adaptable and achieve greater success over time.

3. **Summarize clear steps**

Find the specific actions you need to perform after learning the techniques, and record them. The tasks at hand and their due dates must be defined with precision. Having a goal in mind will change your perspective and help you work towards it. A positive outlook increases the likelihood that you will take the necessary steps toward your objectives.

Acknowledge the little victories along the way, too. You can credit yourself for taking positive steps toward realizing your dreams by establishing objectives and keeping tabs on progress.

It takes smart spending and deliberate behavior to acquire riches. Whether you're buying bonds or stocks, a piece of real estate, or starting a company, you want to be sure you're making a profit. Never forget that if you take on the "empowerment attitude for riches," you can achieve your objectives and live the life you've always imagined.

1.7 Tips for Becoming Empowered for Wealth

Even in an economic downturn, developing the skills necessary to succeed financially is possible. To cultivate a prosperous outlook, it's important to focus on two key things: imagination and attention.

To achieve wealth, imagine your financial goals as a master artist paints their masterpiece. Focus your attention on positive thoughts and block out the distractions like a skilled musician playing a solo. This powerful combination creates a mindset of abundance that attracts success and prosperity. But don't forget to take specific actions, like investing and educating yourself, to turn your vision into reality.

But imagining wealth alone is not enough. To achieve financial success, you must take specific actions. Here are six steps you can take to move closer to your financial goals:

1. **Do it right**

When you hear the phrase "do it right," it means taking purposeful and intentional action towards your financial goals. This involves avoiding impulsive or reckless decisions that have the potential to hinder your progress or derail you from achieving your objectives.

It's important to clearly understand what you're trying to achieve and why, and to ensure that your actions align with your long-term vision for financial success. This requires discipline, focus, and sometimes patience; it's not always easy to stay the course when faced with obstacles or setbacks.

2. **Visualize your future**

Visualization is one of the most frequent ways individuals employ the Law of Attraction. Imagination and focus are required. Spend time imagining the outcome you want each day and letting yourself believe it is already true.

In addition to focusing your thoughts on what you want rather than what you don't like when you first start visualizing, you should maintain this focus throughout the day. Many need to pay more attention to this step and wonder why their visualization isn't producing results.

3. **Develop a wealthy mindset**

Doing activities that make you feel affluent is another powerful method for acquiring money; similarly, with a growth mindset, you must use a wealthy mindset. What is wrong with these folks? They, for one, don't admit or even consider the possibility that they can't afford some things. They browse sales just like everyone else, but when they find something they want, they buy it regardless of the cost.

4. **Begin your investment journey**

Since you can get started immediately with whatever amount you feel is appropriate, investing is an excellent approach to training your mind to think like a rich person. Investing also teaches you to appreciate the mind-boggling concept of infinite supply. It's lavish thinking to assume you have enough cash on hand because more is on the way. Every wealthy person will attest that having plenty of money is a perk.

5. **Educate yourself about money matters**

Learning as much as possible about personal finance is an underrated tool for gaining economic independence. The more you know about personal finance, the more at ease you'll feel when making decisions about your money. As your comfort level with handling smaller sums grows, you'll have more chances to oversee more significant sums.

Your competence and confidence will grow in tandem with your income. And if you can't retain the money you earn, attracting it in the first place is pointless. Many individuals can acquire substantial wealth yet remain perpetually poor because they need more financial skills to manage it. In other words, could you not join them? Learn as much as you can about personal finance.

6. **Wealthy networking: learn from success**

Time spent in the company of the wealthy might inspire you to achieve your financial goals. Find a prosperous individual and invite them to lunch. You might inquire about the person's path to success and any recommendations they may have for others. Doing so will provide you with invaluable experience and knowledge.

If you cannot do so, consider participating in live seminars, teleseminars, or listening to recorded programs given by successful people. What can't be found online can be found during in-person sessions and seminars. Everyone has a unique background and experiences that are worth hearing about.

In a nutshell, there are many approaches you can take if you want to achieve financial independence. Innovate and keep going with the freedom your imagination gives you. If you have faith in yourself, you can do anything.

Believing in your ability to amass riches is essential to enjoying the perks of affluence. Refrain from settling for mediocre prosperity because you assume tremendous success is out of your reach. So why lower your sights and work on earning an additional $100 every week? The vast majority of individuals can do this, giving them more faith in their ability to think positively about money and create it. Those who believe they deserve prosperity and can imagine themselves as wealthy will attract that prosperity to themselves; it's the law of attraction. You may have opportunity after opportunity to earn riches, but you need to believe in yourself to succeed. Despite feeling that the fight is too much or will never end, you must keep your eye on the prize and not get bogged down in the present.

A quantifiable goal and a clear description of why that goal is essential are crucial steps in achieving your desired financial success. Wishing for financial success is futile. Put your financial goals into writing, and spend some time each day seeing yourself as the owner of that precise sum. Immerse yourself in it and let yourself feel the joy it brings.

MODULE 2: WHAT DO YOU WANT YOUR MONEY TO DO FOR YOU?

Asset and Liability

"You must know the difference between an asset and a liability and buy assets.... Rich people acquire assets. Poor and middle-class people acquire liabilities but think they are assets." Robert Kiyosaki wrote in his book "Rich Dad, Poor Dad".

To borrow Kiyosaki's terminology, an asset is everything that can be sold for a profit. Anything that drains your finances is a liability. Kiyosaki claims the standard error of the working class and the impoverished is investing in liabilities rather than assets. He preaches that all one has to do to get wealth is devote one's whole life to acquiring property.

2.1 What is an asset?

If it generates income, then it's an asset. Many self-proclaimed financial gurus and accountants will give you a complicated mathematical definition of what constitutes an asset, but the truth is that if it isn't making you money, it isn't an asset.

2.2 What is a liability?

A liability may be thought of in the most basic terms as costing you money. Automobiles, trips, clothing, restaurants, takeout, unused subscriptions, and other expenses are typical liabilities.

Looking at a poor person's budget, you will see many liabilities but no assets.

2.3 Asset vs. Liability

If you look at it in this straightforward and realistic way, your house is a liability since it requires regular financial outlays like mortgage payments, property taxes, homeowners insurance, and repairs. Instead of making you money, it takes your money. An item is only an asset if it can be sold for a profit. During the Great Recession, many homeowners learned that their home might be a liability if they were forced to sell it in a foreclosure, short sale, or at a loss.

Conversely, a rental property may be an asset if you manage it well and bring in more rent than you spend on monthly maintenance and repairs. Net operating income is the money left over after paying monthly bills. It's valuable because of that fact.

There is a simple test: if the real estate pays you money (rent minus expenses and mortgage payments, leaving positive cash flow), it's an asset.

If you pay out money for your real estate, such as a cottage you buy for your use, and pay realty taxes, insurance, utilities, maintenance, repairs, and mortgage payments (even if you rent it a tiny bit on Airbnb but still have an overall negative cash flow), it's a liability.

That's why your own house is not an asset. The cost of carrying it, over what you could rent the accommodation for is negative cash flow. In the long run, values will increase more than the negative cash flow you have incurred for years.

Studies have proven that the stock market will grow your investment better than real estate. But that only applies to real estate from which you derive no cash flow, like your house.

But if you compare the stock market to income property, where you're getting cash flow plus growth in value, income property is much superior.

So, what to do about owning a house? It's more expensive than renting in the short run, but cheaper than renting in the long run if it goes through market value growth periods. There are many periods where values stay flat and drop, even drastically, somewhere.

The answer? There are other intangible benefits to owning your home. Pride of ownership. Sense of place. Feeling in control. Less congestion.

If you want to own it, include some rental aspects. Rent out a basement apartment. Rent out a room. Rent out your garage. Rent it all out when you go on vacation. List it for use in a movie. Install solar panels. Grow pricey herbs and mushrooms in the backyard and sell them at a local market or to gourmet restaurants. Rent your driveway space for parking if you're near significant events or subway stops; put a trailer in your backyard and rent it out. You get the idea. Make the most of whatever you've got.

The real estate itself is an asset on the balance sheet.

However, unless you paid for it outright (i.e., didn't have to borrow to acquire it), it will also create a liability on the balance sheet for whatever amount was borrowed. If you bought a piece of real estate for $100,000 and put $20,000 down, you'd have to borrow $80,000 to finance the rest. This would look like the following:

Assets = Equity + Liabilities

$100,000 (Real Estate) = $20,000 (Down Payment) + $80,000 (Loan)

Your real estate can either be an asset that brings in money or a liability that drains your finances, depending on how you use it. Let's figure it out by examining the examples below.

Renting vs. owning a home is a big decision that requires careful consideration of many factors. Both options have advantages and disadvantages, and weighing them all before deciding is important.

Advantages of Renting:

- Flexibility: Renters can move without the burden of selling a property.
- Low maintenance: Renters are not responsible for the upkeep and maintenance of the property, which can save money and time.
- No property taxes: Renters do not have to pay property taxes.
- Lower upfront costs: Renting typically requires only a security deposit and the first month's rent, whereas buying a home requires a significant down payment and closing costs.

Disadvantages of Renting:

- No equity: Renters do not gain equity in their rented property.
- Limited control: Renters have limited control over the property and may be unable to make certain modifications.
- No tax benefits: Renters do not receive the same tax benefits as homeowners.
- Rent increases: Rent can increase over time, making it difficult for renters to budget for the long term.

Advantages of Owning:

- Building equity: By paying a monthly mortgage, homeowners build property equity.
- Tax benefits: Homeowners may claim certain tax deductions, such as mortgage interest.
- Appreciation: The home's value can be appreciated over time, which can result in a profitable sale.
- Sense of stability: Owning a home can provide stability and permanence.

Disadvantages of Owning:

- Enormous upfront costs: Purchasing a home requires a significant down payment and closing costs.
- Maintenance and repairs: Homeowners are responsible for the upkeep and maintenance of the property, which can be costly.
- Property taxes: Homeowners must pay property taxes.
- Lack of flexibility: Homeowners may need more flexibility to move as quickly as renters, as they must first sell the property.

Whether to rent or own a home is a personal decision that depends on individual circumstances and priorities. Renting can offer more flexibility and lower upfront costs, while owning a rental-producing home can provide long-term financial benefits and stability. It's essential to weigh the pros and cons of each option and consider factors like your financial situation, lifestyle, and plans before making a decision.

The table below breaks down renting vs owning. Based on this breakdown, you can determine what is best for you at any given time.

Renting	Owning
Monthly Rent: $2,000	Monthly Mortgage: $2,000

Renting	Owning
Security Deposit: $2,000	Down Payment: $40,000 (20% of the home value of $200,000)
First Month Rent: $2,000	Closing Costs: $6,000
Total Move-in Costs: $4,000	Total Move-in Costs: $46,000
No Property Taxes	Property Taxes: $2,000 (assuming 1.5% of home value)
No Repairs or Maintenance Costs	Repairs and Maintenance Costs: $500 per month
No Equity Building	Equity Building: $200 per month (assuming home value appreciation of 3% per year)
No Tax Benefits	Tax Benefits: $300 per month (assuming mortgage interest deduction)
Potential Rent Increases	Potential Appreciation in home value
Limited Control over the property	Complete Control over the property
Flexibility to move	Less flexibility to move (need to sell the property)
No rental income	Rental Income: $2,500 per month (assuming renting out the property)
No depreciation tax benefits	Depreciation Tax Benefits: $200 per month (assuming depreciation of 3% per year)

Note: This table assumes a home value of $200,000, a 3% appreciation rate, a 1.5% property tax rate, and a 4% mortgage interest rate. It also assumes that the renter stays for five years and the homeowner stays for five years. Additionally, it believes the homeowner can rent the property for $2,500 monthly[1]. We can see here in this example that owning a home and using it as an investment will be more profitable over time versus renting.

As a rule of thumb, unless capital appreciation is equal to or more than the cost of borrowing, there is very little chance of making a significant return on real estate. People should understand the economics of scale before entering real estate investing. To plan your exit, you must understand the current market dynamics and the future. On the contrary, it could become a massive liability if bought at the "wrong time" and at the "wrong price".

Creating a Real Estate Business Plan for Investment Success

Real estate investment success only happens slowly and is likely to occur with careful consideration and preparation. A real estate business plan can be your guide to successful investment.

Developing a successful real estate investment portfolio begins with a well-thought-out business strategy. Creating an effective business strategy will require careful consideration of several factors. This includes future objectives, business ideals, financial plans, and more. A well-thought-out business strategy can lay the groundwork for seamless operations and a bright future for your investment career.

1 **These values are for illustration purposes only and should not be considered investment advice. It is essential to consult with a tax and financial professional to understand the tax benefits and implications of owning a rental property.*

Why Create a homeownership Business Plan?

Failing to plan is planning to fail. Your business plan is the GPS for success. Instead of wandering, push towards your goals and objectives with clear direction.

The numbers back this up!

Realizing your lifelong goal of owning your own house is not out of the question! In 2021, 65 percent of people living in the United States had their own houses; you can do the same thing. 16 percent of homeowners are either Generation Z or millennials, although the typical age of first-time homebuyers has risen for several reasons over the last several years. The question is, how did they get there? Typically, by engaging in cautious homeownership business planning, if you get a head start on your planning, you'll be able to get the keys to your first house much faster. The following advice will help you successfully start on the road to homeownership.

The home-buying process might be scary. For many individuals, purchasing a house is the most significant financial transaction they will ever undertake. Because it's an extensive choice that involves a lot of time and effort, you need to know exactly what's involved and how to proceed. There are benefits and drawbacks to both purchasing and renting a property. Start the house-buying process by weighing the advantages of owning a home against the disadvantages of staying in a rented apartment; review back to the table for an analysis of renting vs owning. Homeownership may be the best option for those with a strong desire to own their property, are prepared to maintain their property, and expect to stay in the same neighborhood for at least five years, provided they have the financial means to do so.

Steps to becoming a homeowner within 5 years

Step 1: Make a budget and start saving now!

Determine how much of a mortgage payment you can afford based on your present income. To assist you in determining a price range to aim for, you can use an affordability calculator. Establish a target amount for your down payment savings and calculate how much money you'll need to put away each month to reach that goal. You can save more quickly if you designate a particular amount of money from each paycheck to be set aside and transferred into a savings account established only for this purpose. Now is the time to start putting money down for a home if you still need to do so. The larger the down payment you can make on a property, the cheaper your subsequent monthly payments will be. For example, a down payment of 20 percent of a property priced at $250,000 would be $50,000. For the next five years, you should put aside around $830 every month, which is a sum that could be difficult to set aside. Even if a down payment of 20 percent is unnecessary, making one of any amount less than that might result in a higher interest rate and mortgage insurance added to your monthly cost.

Step 2: Create a Market Overview

The next step is to look up the average sale price of homes in your chosen ZIP code, the number of homes bought or sold in the area over the past year, and the number of properties that were taken off the market without being purchased by visiting the United States Census Bureau's website, Realtor.com's housing research, and the Department of Housing and Urban Development's website. Ask a realtor.

Consider how the country's more significant economic and cultural variables could affect property prices, sales, and market changes in these areas. Consider how local restrictions and laws might influence your research.

For your real estate investment strategy, here are some questions to ask about the market:

- How have home prices fluctuated recently, and how have they done so historically?
- During the previous five years, have homebuying trends changed in any way?
- How do the region's economic factors affect the present market?
- Is there any new business or construction in the region that might impact real estate prices?
- In the next 5–10 years, would my investments be affected by any financial, economic, or cultural factors?

Improve the state of your credit:

Lenders will be aware of your less-than-stellar credit history, which may result in a higher interest rate or possibly a rejection of your application for a house loan. It takes seven years for negative markers like charge-offs, collection accounts, and even late payments to disappear from your report. It may take a few months to several years for your credit score to rebound after being negatively impacted. You won't be able to speed up this process, but there are certain things you can do to make sure the years that are closest to the present on your report are accurate. From this point forward, always pay your bills on time, and be sure you pay them altogether. Reduce your current debt until your credit is used for less than 30 percent of its capacity. You should routinely examine your credit report and cooperate with the institutions maintaining it to correct inaccuracies.

Reevaluate, yet continue in the same direction:

In a few years, a lot can change; for example, you might have gained a new family member or been promoted at work. If everything stays the same, you should stay within your planned amount of savings each month. If your anticipated household budget needs to be adjusted upwards or downwards, you should reevaluate the amount you set aside each month to remain on track. Do you and your significant other intend to purchase a property together? Make sure that you and your partner have the same understanding of the timeline and the costs involved. When deciding whether or not to grant a mortgage to a couple, the lender will look at the applicant with the lower credit score. Your chances of being approved for the best possible interest rates are directly proportional to how good your scores are.

Get focused

Bring the focus closer. Your dream of investing in a house has been nothing more than a dream. Now is the time to start refining your focus, developing your list of wants and requirements for a home, looking at suitable communities, and chatting with friends and family about their experiences with local real estate agents. The closer you get to the moment you purchase a property, the more crucial it is to understand the scope of future costs. You will need money for the down payment, relocation expenses, and finalizing the mortgage deal. To avoid unpleasant financial surprises, create a checklist of all financial obligations as soon as possible. At this point, you'll need to be even more frugal to achieve the savings objectives you've set for yourself.

Get the answers to these questions about yourself:

- What am I looking for in terms of real estate?
- In what ways am I special in terms of my background, skills, or experience?

Get in the shopping mood.

This year will be a busy one for you, with the culmination being the acquisition of your investment property. Gather all the necessary paperwork to submit with your mortgage application (tax returns, pay stubs, etc.). Get pre-approved for a mortgage. Pick a real estate agent to work with you. Examine the options of at least three different mortgage lenders, evaluating the interest rates and costs. Start looking for a place to purchase.

Step 3: Define Your Mission Statement

The excitement and tension start when you look for an investment property. Because purchasing a house may be an emotionally taxing experience, having a well-defined financial plan and clear goals is essential before looking at available properties. Make a distinction between the elements of a house that are essential for you and those you'd like to have but can live without. Then, stick to your priorities while remaining within a price range that is manageable for you. You will only need part of the five years to be ready to purchase a house, particularly if you already have a solid credit history and some money stashed away in an emergency fund. However, considerable forward-looking preparation is going to be required for this. If you get a head start on your practices, you will be able to realize your goal of becoming a homeowner much more quickly.

Finding the home for you

Prospective homebuyers have a wide range of options to choose from. There are unlimited floor plans in a wide range of residences. However, before you start shopping for a home, take some time to assess your wants and requirements.

Evaluating needs and desires

Knowing the difference between what you want and need is crucial to making the home-buying process more accessible. List everything you've always desired in a house as a starting point. This is a "wish list," so don't be afraid to add everything you want. Next, write a second list of all the amenities you need in a house—things you cannot live without. Take into account the following points:

- Size: Determine how many bedrooms and bathrooms you need to live comfortably. 'Size matters. The school board oversees the district, and property values rise more quickly in areas with excellent public schools. Your children's educational requirements must be considered while choosing a school district.
- Location: If you have to commute to work, school, or other often-visited locations, the location of your house may be an essential consideration.
- Amenities: Exceptional amenities of the house (such as a fireplace or terrace) and community services are included (such as a public library, nearby stores, and parks). Most first-time homebuyers can't afford the house of their dreams, so making a realistic list of requirements is essential. Once you've figured out what you want in a home, it's time to begin searching.

When developing your mission statement, understand that the mission you develop now may have different visions. Each vision attributes to the mission. Although your vision may change, your mission remains the same.

Step 4: SWOT Analysis

When developing a strategy for real estate investment, using a SWOT analysis is one of the most crucial components. Using a SWOT analysis, you can determine the advantages, disadvantages, opportunities, and threats of purchasing a house. The SWOT analysis is often used to evaluate how the process of becoming a homeowner progresses and what aspects need to be changed. However, it can also be used to determine how a particular project is going. Decision-making can be sped up and improved using a SWOT analysis.

A SWOT analysis of buying a home can be used to make critical strategic choices and achieve company goals. The following are the four components of a SWOT analysis when purchasing a home:

1. Strength
2. Weakness
3. Opportunity
4. Threat

What is a SWOT analysis for real estate? Let's review the breakdown:

Strengths:

- Real estate can be a stable and profitable investment.
- There is a constant demand for housing.
- Real estate offers the potential for appreciation in value.
- Real estate can provide a steady stream of rental income.

Weaknesses:

- Real estate can be expensive to get into.
- There can be a lot of competition in specific markets.
- Transactions can be time-consuming and complex.
- The value of real estate can be affected by local and national economic conditions.

Opportunities:

- The low-interest rate environment makes it easier to obtain financing.
- Demographics such as an aging population and the growth of remote work can drive demand for housing.
- Government policies, such as tax incentives, can be favorable to real estate investors.
- Technology advancements make it easier to research and find properties to invest in.

Threats:

- Economic downturns can lead to a decrease in property values.

- Natural disasters can cause damage to properties.
- Government regulations and policies can change, potentially impacting the real estate market.
- Changes in zoning laws and building codes can affect the value of properties.

The Buying a Home SWOT Analysis must distinguish short- and long-term threats. Threats that have immediate ramifications must be handled as a matter of urgency to prevent any damage. Even after dealing with the current dangers, long-term problems may still need to be addressed.

When developing your SWOT analysis, use these statements to determine where you are in the process. If the strengths & opportunities outweigh the weakness and threats, you're in a good position. If it is the other way around, then you have a bit more work to do. However, the opportunity to learn still exists. Whether buying a home for personal use or as an investment, developing a business plan acts as your guide to owning a home.

MODULE 3:
TYPES OF REAL ESTATE INVESTMENTS

3.1 Exploring the Dynamics of Real Estate Investing

Real estate investment involves the purchase of property with the aim of generating a return on the investment. There are various types of real estate investments, each possessing distinct characteristics and potential for returns.

1. Residential Real Estate Investment: Residential real estate investment entails acquiring single-family homes, duplexes, triplexes, and apartment buildings to rent out to tenants. This type of investment offers a consistent rental income stream and the possibility of the property appreciating in value. It is suitable for investors who prefer to be actively involved and can either manage the property themselves or hire a property management company.

2. Commercial Real Estate Investment: Commercial real estate investment involves purchasing properties such as office buildings, warehouses, retail centers, and hotels for business leasing. This type of investment provides reliable rental income and the potential for the property to appreciate in value. It also presents opportunities for investors to develop the property and enhance its value.

3. Industrial Real Estate Investment: Industrial real estate investment is similar to commercial real estate investment but focuses on properties like factories and warehouses primarily used for manufacturing and distribution. This type of investment offers a consistent rental income stream and the potential for the property's value to appreciate. Investors can also explore options for property development to increase its overall value.
4. Retail Real Estate Investment: Real estate investment is akin to commercial real estate investment, but it centers on properties such as shopping centers and strip malls leased to retailers. This type of investment provides a stable rental income and the potential for the property's value to appreciate. Additionally, investors can leverage opportunities to develop the property and augment its value.
5. Land Investment: Land investment involves acquiring land to hold it for future appreciation or development. This type of investment carries some risk as land values fluctuate significantly based on factors like zoning changes, economic conditions, and financing availability. However, land investments can yield substantial returns if the land is developed and its value increases over time.
6. REITs (Real Estate Investment Trusts): REITs are investment vehicles that enable individuals to invest in a diversified portfolio of real estate properties. Typically managed by professional real estate managers, REITs offer a steady stream of income and the potential for the properties' value to appreciate.
7. Crowdfunding Real Estate Investment: Crowdfunding real estate investment is a relatively new approach that allows individuals to invest small amounts of money in real estate projects. This type of investment enables individuals to participate in real estate ventures that might otherwise have been financially out of reach. Crowd-

funding real estate investment also allows investment in projects beyond one's immediate area.

There is a wide range of real estate investments, each with potential benefits and drawbacks. Investors should consider their objectives and level of comfort with risk before deciding on a real estate investing strategy. Research the market and consult experts before making any financial commitments. Investing in real estate may be a terrific way to amass money over time, but only if you take the time to research the market and weigh the pros and cons of a SWOT analysis.

In the past half-century, real estate has risen in prominence as a preferred means of financial accumulation. We'll review some of the best alternatives for individual investors and the benefits of becoming involved.

Being a landlord is an excellent option for investors to generate real estate money. Home "flippers" seek properties they believe are underpriced, purchase them, and then improve them to sell them at a higher price.

REITs allow investors to have exposure to the real estate market without taking on property ownership, management, or financing responsibilities.

The Washington Post reports that 80% of the population makes do with just 3% of the country's general geographical area. With 28.7% of the land, the federal government is the largest landowner. After that come the top 100 private landowners, who own almost as much land as New England (40.2 million acres).

3.2 Types of Real Estate

3.2.1 Residential Real Estate

Homes, townhomes, apartments, buildings, and second homes rented out to individuals or families for residential usage are all considered residential properties. The lease they sign with you will determine how long they can remain in the property. In the United States, home leases typically last for twelve months.

3.2.2 Commercial Real Estate

Skyscrapers and office buildings are two types of commercial real estate. You may develop a modest office building with private rooms with the money you've saved. And then, you could rent them out to businesses, nonprofits, and single proprietors, all of whom would be happy to pay you money in exchange for using your property.

Standard methods of investing in commercial real estate include the ones listed below.

- Real estate investment trusts (REITs)
- Owning and operating a business property
- Crowdfunding

The investor participating in a real estate investment trust (REIT) or a crowdfunded project does not possess the authority to actively participate in or attain full ownership of the project. Commercial property ownership and management are possible for people who can devote more time and resources to the endeavor.

REITs (pronounced "reets") are a kind of real estate investment fund that trades like a stock but invests directly in properties, mainly commercial buildings. A person's retirement or stock portfolio may include real estate investment trusts. Researching these funds is as simple as looking them up on TD Ameritrade or Charles Schwab since they get the same ratings as equities.

3.2.3 Industrial Real Estate

Warehouses and factories are both standard features of industrial real estate. These structures are ideal for laboratories, factories, warehouses, and shipping hubs. Commercial real estate might include systems used for product distribution. Different regulations govern zoning, building, and selling according to the classification.

The land encompasses both undeveloped spaces and operational farms and ranches. The term "vacant land" may refer to any area not currently used for commercial or residential purposes, such as farms or ranches. Raw land and other natural resources like mineral, water, and air rights are examples of this investment.

3.3 Four Factors Affect Real Estate Investing

Like every other type of investment, real estate investing is affected by various factors. Some have a direct and noticeable effect; for example, rising interest rates lead to lower property values. Others, such as changing demographics, have a less focused impact that affects values over time.

Four factors affect real estate investing:

1. **Economy**

The overall state of the economy plays a crucial role in real estate investing, but its impact varies depending on the type of investment. In a thriving economy, real estate values generally experience growth, while they tend to decline in a sluggish economy. However, it's important to note that real estate investments can still thrive in any economic climate, and some even perform exceptionally well during downturns.

Economic fluctuations do not affect different sectors within the real estate investment landscape equally. Certain types of investment properties are particularly susceptible to the effects of an economic slowdown. Consequently, real estate investment trusts (REITs) and funds specializing in these sectors may witness significant price decreases. Nevertheless, well-managed funds have the opportunity to acquire distressed commercial properties at lower costs, holding onto them in anticipation of the eventual economic recovery.

During a sluggish economy, specific types of real estate investments tend to retract. These include:

- Hotels
- New home construction
- Shopping centers

Other types of real estate investments thrive in a down economy. For example, discount retailers see an uptick in sales as people adjust their budgets. Industries, which include casinos, also flourish as the economy worsens. Other recession-resistant property types are self-storage facilities and mobile home parks.

2. **Interest Rates**

Interest rates play a crucial role in the real estate market as they directly influence the affordability of property purchases, particularly in the residential real estate sector. This aspect holds significant importance for both landlords and house flippers. When interest rates are low, the cost of obtaining a mortgage decreases, prompting more individuals to consider buying property. The increased demand resulting from lower rates can, in turn, drive up real estate prices. However, when interest rates start to rise, mortgage costs increase, reducing the likelihood of prospective homeowners making purchases. As a consequence, this decrease in demand can eventually lead to a decline in real estate prices. That can be a double bonus for landlords because any extra mortgage costs can be passed on to tenants through higher rent.

Rates also affect other types of real estate investments. For example, REITs (real estate investment trusts) offer a steady yield (sort of like interest on a bond). When interest rates drop, those yields look better, so demand for REITs and their prices increase too. On the flip side, when interest rates rise, they can outpace that yield, making REITs look less attractive and lowering their market value. Those price fluctuations matter more if you're buying or selling— not if you're sitting back and collecting the income from your REIT investments.

3. **Demographics**

Regarding real estate, people matter, and that's what demographics are all about. Demographics are statistics about the population and its subgroups that help describe group behaviors. Demographic factors include things like:

- Age
- Income level
- Marital status
- Occupation
- Family size

Substantial changes in population composition can have far-reaching effects on real estate markets, especially for residential rental properties, for many years. Examples include the potential for significant shifts in the housing market brought on by the retirement of baby boomers. About 40% of US homeowners are baby boomers, and as they age, they may sell their larger family homes in favor of lower-maintenance condos. The potential increase in the supply of single-family homes on the market could have notable implications. While a decline in prices would undoubtedly have adverse effects on current homeowners, investors in the housing market would view it as a favorable development, presenting them with new and attractive opportunities.

Looking ahead, it is worth considering that the working-age population is projected to grow by approximately 28.52 percent by the year 2050. This growth suggests that home prices may experience a steady upward trajectory over the next 35 years. However, it is important for the United States and the global economy to navigate and avoid any potential financial crises to maintain this positive outlook.

To forestall another crisis, the federal government of the United States must impose stricter regulations.

According to ATTOM Data, a leader in real estate data nationwide, 62 percent of the real estate market growth will be heading south. They predict more people will move to states like Texas, Georgia, and Arizona thanks to warmer weather, more affordable housing, and job availability.

Other boomer-related trends could include shifts away from colder climates to more temperate areas, increased demand for independent living communities, and a swing toward more convenient urban-style locations—all important factors for real estate investors to consider.

4. **Government Actions**

Federal, state, and local governments can impact demand for real estate and property values. They can boost demand in an area by offering tax deductions, tax credits, and subsidies to drive investor interest. They can steer policy and legislation for a specific effect, like the introduction of the first-time homebuyer credit in 2009, which encouraged home sales in a sagging real estate market.

In 2017, the Tax Cuts and Jobs Act (TCJA) implemented a maximum tax deduction limit of $10,000 for state and local taxes (SALT), encompassing income taxes and property taxes at the state and local levels. This new cap can potentially discourage prospective homeownership and significantly favor both direct and indirect residential rental property owners. Plus, the SALT cap doesn't affect real estate investors, who can still deduct the total amount of taxes paid to support rental properties.

The TCJA also created tax-advantaged Opportunity Zones to attract long-term investment in distressed areas and spur development and job creation. There are designated OZs in every state and five US territories. Assets must be made through Qualified Opportunity Funds (QOFs), holding companies set up to allow investment in eligible properties. Potential tax benefits include:

- Defer tax on prior gains until 2026. That means if someone sells the stock and makes a $100,000 profit, then puts that money in a QOF, they don't have to pay taxes on the profit now.
- Exclude 10% of that prior gain forever if they hold the OZ property for at least five years and 15% if they hold it for seven years.
- Investors who keep QOF assets for a minimum of 10 years won't be subjected to capital gains tax on earnings from sales.

As you might imagine, OZs have real estate investors across the US very excited— but the rules are brand-new, and no one has tested them out yet. Proceed with caution.

Learn more about Opportunity Zones on the IRS website (www.irs.gov).

3.4 Four Reasons To Invest In Real Estate

1. Build Your Fortune

There are four primary benefits to investing in real estate and one possible drawback. Profit in real estate is often made via appreciation, or the rise in the value of a property achieved upon sale, whether residential or commercial, and the capitalization rate. Real estate may increase in value primarily due to its location, development, and upgrades.

2. It's Real

Real estate is a tangible investment alternative to stocks, bonds, and mutual funds. It is there for your eyes, hands, and feet to experience. It's not virtual, like bitcoin or stock options; it's not limited to the pages of a balance sheet or the trading floors of financial centers; it's real. In contrast to stocks and bonds, which would be worthless in a market collapse, you would still have something of value if their present market value fell to zero. Even if the property is weak on the market, you may still put it to good use. You may build a home there or use it for other services (such as growing food). Indirect real estate investments are also grounded in tangible assets, which helps them maintain a steady value despite market fluctuations.

3. Limited Supply

Apart from stocks and bonds, there are always other investing options. Increased stock issuance is an option for corporations. Governments and enterprises may issue new bonds to the market to raise capital. Land may be repurposed, but it can't be manufactured from anything. When there is a lack of available properties and prices increase, bidding wars for housing are frequent. Many interested parties can compete to sell a single property by offering ever-higher prices.

4. More Control

When you own real property, you have greater influence over your investment than if you possessed stock (a tiny share of a firm) or other paper-based assets. For example, you may do things to make your home more valuable, like purchasing a new roof. Increase rent and target more financially stable renters to increase revenue. The trade-off is that you must keep closer tabs on your investment. You'll have to keep up with routine maintenance and repairs or hire someone else, such as a property manager.

3.5 Real Estate Investment Strategies

The following exit strategies apply to every type of real estate asset class (residential, multifamily, apartments, commercial office space, industrial, and land). Although you're likely more interested in fixing and flipping, or even wholesaling, having a fundamental grasp of all three is still beneficial.

3.5.1. Buying and Holding

As a generally accepted method of portfolio diversification, this is a frequent real estate investing strategy. When investing in real estate, the "buy and hold" approach means just that: purchasing a home to keep it as an investment for at least five years. It's not like you're buying an investment property to "flip" it and then selling it off quickly for a profit.

Long-term real estate investors sometimes use a strategy known as "buy and hold," in which they make a single significant acquisition and then sit on it for years. Renting out the property until it can be sold helps finance a "buy and hold," until owner plans to sell.

The idea of "buying low and selling high" is straightforward. This is a long-term investment strategy in real estate employed by investors to protect their wealth from inflation and increase their monthly cash flow. It's an excellent method to gain cash, too.

A robust economy typically results in a yearly increase of around 6% in real estate values. To be sure, only in the most desirable areas—those with clean streets, secure neighborhoods, and convenient access to both work and entertainment—can one hope for even a moderate appreciation rate. If you include rental income, paying off debt, asset appreciation, and tax deductions, you may expect a reliable, above-average return on investment.

The investment property is rented out during the "holding" phase. The rental income is where the return on investment lies. If executed properly, the buy-and-hold approach to investing in real estate may result in short- and long-term benefits.

The buy-and-hold real estate investment strategy is how to invest in real estate if you're a beginner. This is mainly because it is one of the more straightforward strategies for first-time investors than the fix-and-flip strategy, which requires experience to spot the right distressed properties. It's also a favored strategy among experienced property investors looking to build wealth over time from property appreciation and equity buildup.

Types of Buy-and-Hold Real Estate

Different types of buy-and-hold real estate properties offer various opportunities for income generation. To maximize your investment strategy, it is essential to identify the specific type of property or rental strategy you prefer. Here are some examples:

1. Turnkey Real Estate:

Investing in turnkey real estate involves purchasing a move-in ready property with professional property management in place and often with existing tenants. This hassle-free approach allows you to "turn the key" and immediately have a substantial investment property.

2. Vacation Rental Property:

The vacation rental market has experienced significant growth recently. Investing in short-term rentals can be lucrative if you make well-timed and informed decisions.

3. Single-Family Home:

Single-family homes are commonly used for traditional long-term rentals. Investing in a single-family home allows beginners to grasp the fundamentals of the real estate industry. With a single rental unit and one tenant, it simplifies management.

4. Multi-Family Home:

For those seeking more substantial opportunities, investing in a multi-family home is an excellent buy-and-hold real estate strategy. These properties consist of buildings with two to four housing units. Although they are usually more expensive than single-family homes, multi-family homes offer higher rental income potential by renting out multiple units to multiple tenants. This type of investment can provide solid cash flow and expedite the growth of your investment portfolio.

5. Commercial Real Estate:

The buy-and-hold real estate investment strategy extends beyond residential properties. Investors can explore opportunities in commercial real estate by acquiring properties such as office buildings or retail stores for business purposes. However, it's important to note that commercial real estate investing can be more intricate, particularly for beginners. Thorough research and understanding of this strategy are crucial before venturing into commercial real estate investments.

Top Picks for Buy-and-Hold Real Estate Investing Success

When investing in real estate, one of the most critical factors is picking the correct neighborhood. Investors looking to purchase and keep a home should focus on areas with strong rental demand and the potential for a price increase. The potential losses of an investment will be reduced as a result (namely, vacancy rates or property depreciation). Before settling on a specific location for a buy-and-hold real estate investment, comprehensive market research should be performed.

Fortunately, investors can use a few indicators to pinpoint promising real estate areas. Keep an eye out for regions experiencing employment growth and industrial expansion. Find out which corporations have established local offices and are drawing the most local talent. The next metric to keep an eye on, population expansion, will be affected accordingly. Be on the lookout for growing areas to ensure your buy-and-hold investment property will be occupied and continue to appreciate. Look at demographic shifts to gauge market expansion rates. Finally, focus on cost, as it may affect both your ability to make an initial investment during market growth. As a whole, these indicators suggest a robust housing market.

80/20 Rule

Dr. Joseph M. Juran, a quality control manager, discovered a groundbreaking universal concept in the late 1940s that he termed the "vital few and trivial many." One of the main points was that most outcomes emerge from very few inputs. A portion of his findings drew inspiration from the statistical research conducted by Italian economist Vilfredo Pareto, who discovered that a mere 20% of Italians possessed 80% of the nation's wealth. Yet as luck would have it, the widely accepted idea was dubbed Pareto's Principle rather than Juran's Law. It's often referred to as "the 80/20 Rule" these days.

The principle of the 80/20 rule emphasizes that 20% of your efforts yield 80% of your results, making it a highly valuable guideline to abide by. It's all about making the most of your time and energy. The goal is to get the best possible outcomes. Maintaining concentration is critical.

Success requires focusing more than hard work, years of experience, or raw talent. If you study the most successful people in any area, you will see that they are very focused; more importantly, you will notice that they focus on the things that matter the most. They have a keen awareness of when crucial decisions must be made. Gaining that concentration is essential to making it as a real estate investor. The effects of such concentration may be subtle at first, but they will increase dramatically later.

The most successful real estate investors always keep three fundamental factors in mind. Every investment strategy has three essential components: criteria, terms, and a network. They will be referred to as "CTN" for short.

The Three Areas Of Focus

Criteria: What You Buy

Criterion is the first of the three. Buying decisions are based on criteria. Such criteria are the basis for your property search. While looking for a new opportunity, your criteria will be the factors you highlight in your decision making. Does the building house a single household or many families? Does it contain the necessary fixtures and conveniences to be resold or rented? Where is it primarily situated? Your criteria are the fundamental characteristics of the items that cannot be compromised. They are an essential part of your overall investment plan.

Real estate investors may save time and money by using criteria to focus their search on the properties offering the best return on investment with the lowest possible risk. While searching for a home, it's always best when the one you locate meets all your criteria. See your criteria as a "filter for opportunities," screening out the undesirables while admitting the desirables. Flawed criteria (or the lack of any criteria) have been the undoing of many would-be real estate investors, just as excellent criteria are the bedrock of successful investment. Ultimately, criteria are about locating reliable value, which is why they should be the primary focus of every property investor.

Terms: How You Buy It

When an opportunity meets the necessary criteria, it may be converted into a transaction by agreeing to the appropriate terms. Once a property has passed your criteria, its present and future worth will be established by the terms. Various aspects of a real estate transaction, ranging from the purchase price and down payment to the interest rate and closing costs, encompass a wide array of terms and conditions. It can be agreed that the area where the most outstanding value can be generated, even from relatively modest initial conditions, is in the terms. Depending on the situation, a more proficient negotiator of terms might increase your equity, boost your cash flow, or do both.

It involves calculating the sum required to purchase a property, the closing costs, and the expected income. A real estate investor's second area of concentration is the terms, which are concerned with the maximization of financial value.

Making money on terms can be done without having the negotiating skills of Roger Dawson or Donald Trump. Getting the most out of any trade requires a thorough awareness of the monetary underpinnings involved and a systematic approach. Knowing when to walk away from a situation is also essential. Remember that the money you earn is on the way in, not the way out. Instead of purchasing less than you need and expecting the market to rescue you, you are buying what you need and letting the market do the rest. Getting fair terms when you buy is essential.

Network: Who Helps You – Develop your Power Team

When investing, your network is who you rely on for assistance. As you explore the factors that have the greatest impact on real estate investment, you will discover that the network emerges as a surprising frontrunner. Most people imagine an individual investor who is also an entrepreneur who scours the city in search of investment opportunities. Despite this, investors repeatedly thanked the many people who played a role in their success throughout the investigation.

These individuals were fortunate to have connections who facilitated their access to opportunities, provided mentorship, helped them navigate property acquisition and management, and even offered services that enabled them to accomplish more in less time. In business, leveraging competent assistance is a key factor that empowers individuals to achieve greater outcomes than they could on their own.

You'll want to hire various professionals, including real estate brokers, contractors, and property managers. Although it is the third component listed, your network is the most important to your success as an investor since you will depend on its members to help you begin your profession in a secure, reliable, and profitable manner. A real estate investor highlights three crucial areas of focus: criteria, conditions, and network. These aspects encompass what you will acquire, how you will obtain it, and the invaluable support you will receive throughout the journey. It's important to recognize that your network plays a vital role in supporting your investments. At the same time, criteria help identify opportunities, and terms determine the financial aspects. Developing proficiency in these three areas will firmly pave your path toward becoming a sophisticated real estate investor.

3.5.2. Fixing and Flipping

The art of flipping

1. Fix-and-flip
2. Live-in and flip

Here's what a fix-and-flipper does:

- Buys low
- Remodels
- Markets the property
- Sells high

Doing so should be simple. Wrong. The fix-and-flip strategy is the most challenging way out. It calls for the most significant resources, including money, technological know-how, and market awareness. The profit for fix-and-flippers comes from the initial purchase, not the eventual sale. The secret is to buy cheap.

To profit, they need deep discounts on the houses they buy to flip.

1. Repair costs
2. Holding costs (debt service if using leverage, utilities, insurance)
3. Closing costs (title insurance, escrow fees, and loan fees)
4. Commission costs (paid to the buyer's and seller's agents)

Repair prices are of less concern to a wholesale buyer, for instance. They have no plans to repair the house. As a buy-and-hold strategy involves leasing the property, they will not incur any expenses related to the sale or purchase of the property (like commissions or closing fees). Yet, in a tight credit market, eager bidders are plentiful. Hence, an investor who gives the seller financing often pays much less for all these goods. In return for better financing conditions, many purchasers are willing to do much of the work, including making repairs and covering closing expenses. Yet, a fix-and-flipper must think about all four of these factors.

Hence, they need to get the best price for a piece of real estate to profit. How can you get the money, the know-how, and the understanding to renovate and flip houses effectively?

Ways To Flip

1. Fix-and-flip:

You buy a low-priced fixer-upper, make vital improvements, and sell it for a profit.

2. Live-in and flip:

You buy an underpriced property in good structural shape, spruce it up while you live there, and sell it when the property value has increased.

3. Hold and Flip:

It's less popular because you have significantly less control over the outcome. With a hold-and-flip investment, you buy an underpriced property in an expected up-and-coming neighborhood and hold it until property values increase. Without the time to wait or the means to write it off, this would not be a good investment strategy if the increase never materialized.

Most investors go for the straight fix-and-flip—it's what all the shows are about. This is not an arena to enter casually (especially with giant dogs like Zillow joining in), but it is possible to collect big profits with the right approach.

If you're not in a rush, and the property you choose has no issues that make it uninhabitable, the live-in and flip strategy may work better for you. Both systems come with profit and loss potential, but you can tilt the odds in your favor by doing your homework before you buy.

Why Fix-and-Flip?

A fix-and-flip investment could be perfect if you're handy around the house and love DIY home projects. These projects must move quickly to be profitable and require a significant time commitment (even when you don't plan to do most of the work yourself). If you love a challenge, have good credit and a pile of cash, and know your way around tools, this could be an ideal investment opportunity.

Expect your first flip to be a learning experience rather than a profit bonanza (practically, no one makes much money on their initial flip). Pick up as many skills and make as many connections as possible to make your second flip a winning investment.

Why Live-In and Flip?

With this strategy, you buy a house to flip and live in it while doing the repairs. Engaging in this approach can serve as an excellent entry point into house flipping, as it provides ample time to complete tasks and gain valuable experience in the process. Plus, planning to live in the house transforms many of the finances usually associated with house flipping. For example, you can get a regular home mortgage and use traditional homeowners insurance, which can be much less expensive than if you were doing a standard fix-and-flip.

Plus, if you live in a home for at least two years, then capital gains from the sale may be excluded entirely from taxation. That means taxes will only eat a small chunk of your profits, leaving you with more cash to buy your next hold-fix-flip.

Buy Low, Sell High

The idea behind profiting from house flipping is the same as with other investments: sell it for more than you paid, and pocket the difference as profit. According to ATTOM Data, the average house-flipping gross profit (before any expenses were taken into account) for the second quarter of 2018 across the US was $65,520. That sounds like a lot, but it's down about $4,000 from earlier in the year, and the numbers vary widely depending on where you are. Remember that many people lose money or break even when they flip a house, and (again) that's before considering their expenses.

Many factors play into this, but the most important is choosing the right property, followed closely by having an accurate flip budget.

The 70 Percent Rule

To limit the financial downside while maximizing your profit potential when you flip a house, you need to know your costs before you buy a property. First, you need to know how much the property is worth so you don't overpay. Then, it would help if you had a realistic estimate of the repairs and renovations the property needs to be attractive to buyers.

With that information, you can calculate the perfect price for your flip property using the 70% rule.

Savvy real estate investors follow the 70 percent rule to maximize profits.

As per the guideline, it is recommended that the acquisition price not exceed 70% of the after-repair value (ARV), the anticipated selling price of the home after all necessary repairs have been completed, minus the total cost of repairs.

As a simple guideline for establishing an appropriate purchase price based on a property's after-repair worth, investors often rely on the 70% rule (ARV). Real estate flippers usually use the 70% rule, although it may apply to any technique. According to the 70% rule, the maximum amount you should pay is 70% of the item's after-repair value, less the cost to restore it.

Contextual Use: Requiring about $35,000 in repairs to reach its potential selling price of $200,000, the house in question now needs some TLC. The 70% rule states that if you have $200,000, multiply by 70% to reach $140,000, then deduct $35,000 for repairs. Because of this, the highest reasonable offer for this property is $105,000.

Remember that it is best to effectively and quickly determine whether or not more inquiry into a property is warranted. Back of the napkin calculations should never be used when settling a final bill total or deciding whether to invest. If a property meets (or comes close to meeting) the criteria above, doing a more in-depth examination using paper and pencil (or a computer spreadsheet) may be worthwhile. You can't use a general guideline as an excuse to avoid specific research.

3.5.3 Wholesaling

Wholesale real estate involves discovering profitable real estate prospects, entering into a contract to acquire the property, and selling the contract to a third party. In most cases, a wholesaler will never truly own the property they are selling; instead, they will use various promotional methods to locate attractive offers, enter into contracts for them, and then sell those to others for an "assignment fee." Depending on the scope of the transaction, this cost might be much higher than $5,000. The wholesaler's primary function is that of a facilitator, locating and facilitating transactions.

While some wholesalers may choose to sell directly to end consumers, the majority focus on selling to fellow investors, particularly home flippers, who are typically cash buyers. By collaborating with cash purchasers, wholesalers can often receive payment within a short timeframe, ranging from a few days to a few weeks. Additionally, this provides an opportunity to establish valuable connections within the local real estate market.

Due to its image as a simple approach with affordable start-up expenses, wholesaling attracts many new investors. One of the advantages for wholesalers is that they are relieved from the burden of renovation costs, loan fees, dealing with contractors, tenants, banks, and other complexities associated with property ownership. As wholesalers do not actually own the property, they can avoid these challenges and focus solely on the transaction process. While being a successful wholesaler is more complex than many gurus make it seem, it is the most often discussed and widely taught real estate approach.

3.6 Are You Committed to Your Real Estate?

When starting in the real estate investing business, several important issues must be considered. The first and most important thing to consider is how serious you are about having your real estate investment pay off. Sometimes you have to be brutal when dealing with buyers and sellers, but you also have to be very ethical when it comes to the work that has to be done to get a home in sellable shape.

Making real estate work for you requires a genuine commitment, and the reason for this is straightforward. Specific peaks and valleys might be expected. The stock market often undergoes both ups and downs. Similar to how you shouldn't sell all your stocks because of a single poor day, real estate investment is a long-term game that requires patience and perseverance. As a rule, real estate values go up over time. Hence, even if a community's values decline, there is hope that they might rise again.

A "buy and hold investor" anticipates a gradual increase in value. These financiers have an unwavering desire to see their money grow. Some choose to use it as a second home for themselves and their family, while others rent it out to others looking for a holiday.

Profits from short-term rentals may be used to offset some of the expenditures of owning a vacation home, making it possible for a more significant number of individuals to enjoy the luxuries of such a home without the investors who purchase them having to shoulder the whole burden of ownership. This is standard procedure in heavily visited tourist destinations. Those who engage in real estate this way are sometimes called "serious investors", while all real estate buyers must be cautious.

The owners of rental homes must be dedicated to the success of their assets. Unlike other investments, rental properties need regular upkeep to ensure they are in demand among renters. You need to make consistent efforts to maintain these properties well-managed and occupied, to ensure that you are collecting rent regularly, and to prevent the properties from falling into disrepair or being abused by tenants.

Investors often use property management companies to deal with the monotony of collecting rent and other monthly expenses. Whether you have a single rental home or an extensive portfolio, this plan is great. Moreover, if you maintain your rental properties well throughout the years, you'll have something valuable to sell when the time comes. In other words, if you invest for the long term rather than in the here and now, they may more than pay for themselves.

It's crucial to be prepared to devote yourself to making a profit or turning a profit in whatever kind of real estate investing you choose to pursue.

3.7 Tips for a Profitable and Risk-Free deal

Investing in real estate as a novice is never a picnic. It's fraught with peril. Many organizations are peddling real estate investments to beginners, but the issue of how much you can trust them should immediately jump out at you. A new investor might use this guide to learn what is required and what can be disregarded.

Tip # 1: Assess the area

Investigate the neighborhood thoroughly before making a property investment there. Is there anything that would make a family, couple, or individual not want to call this place home? When starting, it's best to focus on options that don't come with any inherent dangers. No matter how stellar a neighborhood's reputation is, it won't be able to afford your mortgage. Property sellers specializing in older buildings, areas with a high concentration of abandoned homes, or locations with a history of criminal activity, such as drug trafficking, should be avoided at all costs. Such dwellings are OK, but stick to the most secure options if you still need to gain experience.

Tip # 2: Trust no one

Consider whether you can afford the home you're interested in buying. The commissions are high. People or corporations have methods of ingeniously gaining your attention and tricking you into accepting their offer. It's not uncommon for people to believe they can afford a particular piece of real estate when, in reality, doing so would put them in a poor house. Only accept the offer if you know how to pay for the home. Bring it down a notch. You'll have a strong intuitive sense of this. Don't let yourself get carried away by reassuring remarks. Go at your speed. Yet, pushing oneself to achieve one's objectives will contribute to learning and growth.

Tip # 3: Ask

For those who are talking a lot, don't be shy about asking a question. Whenever a broker or other person makes a recommendation, you should find out whether they have made any financial investments in the property and/or area in question. If so, it's evidence that the property is a sound investment. But you may want to ask someone else if they still need to put their money where their mouth is. A company's or an agent's offerings may be so compelling that they need no further promotion. In other words, if their services are so great, why have they yet to invest money in advertising them? You should decline the offer until they answer your inquiries.

Tip # 4: Be on your guard

Several individuals will go as far as intentionally misleading others for their gain. Companies' claims of having property masters or gurus are likely to be empty, so you shouldn't fall for them. It would help if you were vigilant in real estate investment to avoid making any choices that might put you in a sticky situation.

If you follow these guidelines, you'll be well on your way to making a more lucrative and less risky transaction. You may get a jump start with these suggestions.

Real Estate requires patience and is not a get-rich-quick scheme. Information is essential to making a profit. In addition to patience, you need strategy and determination. There may be some financial loss up front, but there will be a longer return over time.

Once you have identified your plan of action to mitigate your losses, you'll want to ensure that all of your contracts are in your favor. There are various methods that can be applied when preparing contracts. It starts with your offer. Now that you've done your due diligence, the next step is to translate that information into a contract.

MODULE 4: RESOURCES

4.1. The 5 Big Contract Components

Several critical components of your offer must be decided and added to the contract. Specifically, here are five big decisions you'll need to make to prepare your proposal:

1. **Cash or Financing**

First, you'll need to determine whether you'll offer to purchase the property "all cash" or "financed." This decision will impact several other parts of your offer. If your request is accepted, it will dictate how the seller views the deal throughout the closing process. Generally speaking, an all-cash offer is one where you intend to purchase the property using cash you currently have available in your name (you will likely be asked to prove it). A financed offer is one in which the funds are intended to be borrowed or obtained before the closing.

Sellers tend to be very biased towards all-cash offers, and being able to offer all cash will significantly increase your odds of getting your offer accepted or at least seriously considered. But many sellers (mainly banks if they are offering REOs (Real Estate Owned) are very strict with their definitions. If you can't provide a statement from a bank or brokerage account with your name showing the total amount of the funds available, the seller may not consider you an all-cash buyer. Even if you fully intend to have access to the cash by the closing date (perhaps you're borrowing the money from a family member or are in the process of selling another property), if you can't prove that the cash is in your account at the time of the offer, you run the risk of not being considered a cash buyer, and your dishonesty in the eyes of the seller may cost you the deal.

REOs are often sold at a discount by banks and other lenders.

So, while this may not be what you want to hear, if you can't include a bank statement in your name with the offer, you will make a "financed" offer. On the bright side, when sellers (especially banks) accept a financed offer, they realize that the risks of the deal not closing will be significantly higher. They tend to be more lenient regarding other aspects of the agreement and reopen negotiations should there be inspection items with which the lender takes issue.

It should be noted that banks are concerned about whether an offer is all cash or financing. In a logical sense, "Every offer is an all-cash offer," simply because the seller will always receive a cash payment at the closing, regardless of how the buyer obtained the funds. Of course, from the seller's perspective, an all-cash offer is preferred over a financed offer simply because they don't have to worry about the buyer not being able to get the loan; however, sellers get way too caught up in the terminology as opposed to taking into account all aspects of the offer.

2. **Purchase Price**

Your starting offer price is the next big decision you'll need to make. In some situations, you'll want to start with a low offer that you expect will get negotiated higher. In other cases, you'll want to offer your Best Calculated Offer (BCO) right off the bat.

Depending on the situation, one strategy will likely be more successful.

Starting with a Lowball Offer

The seller probably hasn't had any fair bids in a long time for houses that have been on the market for more than 90 days but have yet to experience a recent price decrease. This implies the seller is more motivated to do a deal to get rid of the property, which is good news for you since you may potentially get a great deal on the house by purchasing it below the asking price and using your BCO. But even though a property has been on the market for a while, you can still start negotiations at 65% or 70% of the list price and work your way up to the total asking price. You may start bargaining at your chosen price when dealing with private vendors.

When making your first offer on a property that has been on the market for an extended period of time, your goal should be to get a counteroffer. This indicates that the seller is willing to negotiate and will at least entertain a low offer. Once you get that first counteroffer, you can be reasonably sure that the seller is motivated and will come off the list price by at least 5-10% if you continue negotiating.

TIP: Specifically regarding REO offers, the seller's first counteroffer will be near or at the total price, while the second counteroffer will generally represent their most significant price reduction. For example, a property is listed at $100,000, and you offer $75,000. Often, the seller will make their first counteroffer near the total price; in this situation, the seller may counter at $97,000 or $98,000. You will then make your first counteroffer. Give in just a bit more than the seller did, perhaps with a counteroffer of $79,000. The seller's subsequent counteroffer will likely represent their most significant price drop, down to $88,000. At this point, you can expect that future counteroffers will be small and that the seller will want to stay relatively close to that $88,000 price. Of course, this is just an example; actual price negotiations will vary wildly based on the property, the seller, and the situation.

Starting with Your Best Calculated Offer:

In other situations, you're more likely to get a property under contract by making your first offer your highest BCO. This situation most commonly arises when buying a publicly marketed property (i.e., on the Multiple Listing Service) that has just been put on the market. It's priced very reasonably, especially if there isn't a lot of competition.

Let's look at an example where an investor is perusing the Multiple Listing Service (MLS). Jennifer saw an REO listing in the same area where she had successfully flipped multiple homes. The asking price was $5,000 less than what she was willing to pay for the property (it was a great deal). She phoned the realtor, assuming there were offers on the property or at least several inquiries about it. However, Jennifer learned that there were no other bids and that the seller was eager to close a deal.

The fact that the realtor said that the seller was motivated indicated that Jennifer likely could have submitted an offer below the list price and still had a reasonable shot at negotiating the deal. So, what did Jennifer do?

She immediately put in an offer over the list price!

Since there was no competition and the seller was motivated, why would she offer more than the asking price? She knew that if she started discussions by providing less than the asking price, the process would take many days to conclude. At that point, additional investors who had missed the listing due to the holiday season would find it and begin placing bids, driving the price even higher. Otherwise, the home may have sold for even more than the asking price, and she would have needed help to afford it.

She calculated that if she made an offer somewhat more than the asking amount, the seller would be more likely to accept it immediately.

On the contrary, she often submits bids at or over the BCO for freshly listed, competitively priced properties where there is intense buyer competition. What if Jennifer's BCO exceeds the retail price? She has no qualms about making an offer more significant than the asking price if she expects competition and if her offer is still reasonable.

You will likely see the phrase "highest and best" often while working with REOs. In real estate parlance, this phrase means "Give me your highest offer". The listing agent (the agent representing the seller) often uses it. This is standard practice when there are numerous interested buyers for a property, and the seller wants to handle all negotiations simultaneously. When the highest and best bids have been presented, the seller will either accept one of the offers or continue negotiations with one of the bidders.

It is very uncommon for the selling agent to claim that there are other bidders who want the highest and best offer, even while the buyer knows or strongly suspects that only one person submitted a proposal. Many investors believe that the "highest and best" game is very immoral when there are no other bids. Remember that the seller is using the highest and best as one of several bargaining tools to maximize the profit from the transaction. And thus, as an investor, you have to deal with it when making offers on properties, even though it may appear immoral (and will surely be bothersome).

Here are a couple of crucial things to keep in mind when you get asked for your highest and best offer:

Just because you're being asked for your best offer doesn't mean you must raise your offer. If your previous offer is the highest you want to go, or if you suspect that your offer is the only offer and you're willing to take a chance, you can feel free to tell the listing agent that your current offer is your highest and best.

Never exceed your BCO just because an agent asks for the highest and best. Even if you know other investors are willing to bid above your BCO, don't get sucked into feeling like you need to go higher. There are always other properties, and it's undoubtedly better to lose one than to get one but have it be a bad deal.

3. Earnest Money:

When dealing with a private seller, the earnest money deposit could be as small as $10 or $100 (in some cases, it could even be $0!). There is no significant downside to giving a small earnest money deposit as a buyer, so when buying from private sellers, always shoot for as little as possible. The significant advantage of a larger deposit is psychological: large amounts of money upfront look very enticing. They may allow you to negotiate better terms on the rest of the deal, such as a lower purchase price.

When dealing with a bank-owned property, you must put down at least $500 in earnest money and possibly more. These days, many banks require at least $1000 in earnest money, and if your offer is an all-cash offer, you will generally be required to put down 10% of the purchase price as earnest money.

TIP: When making an offer on REOs, you will likely be required to provide a personal check for the earnest money when the offer is made. Your agent will probably photocopy the bill and attach a copy to the request. This check, however, WILL NEVER BE CASHED. If the bank decides to accept your offer, you will be asked to provide earnest money in the form of certified funds (a cashier's check, for example), and your check will be returned to you. If you plan to make several simultaneous offers and are concerned about all the personal earnest money checks you'll need to write, ask your agent to use an exact photocopy of your bill for all the offers. Since this check will never be cashed, your agent should be OK with doing this.

4. Closing Costs:

Many new investors (and new homebuyers) don't realize this, but in some areas of the country and for some price levels of houses, it's common for the buyer to ask the seller to pay some or all of the closing costs for them. This is more common for lower-priced houses and buyers getting loans, as these buyers tend to have the least disposable cash and are trying to save as much as possible.

Typically, a buyer may ask a seller to contribute 3-4% (and sometimes as much as 6%) of the transaction price to their closing expenses (the maximum limit that most lenders will allow).

So, when you're the buyer, remember that you have the right to ask the seller to offset some of your upfront costs by having them pay part of your closing costs for you. Remember that when making offers on short sales, the seller generally doesn't have any money to contribute (they can't even pay their mortgage), and the lender generally won't contribute, so don't expect to get any closing costs in this situation. And, when buying REOs, the bank will be a lot more accommodating about paying closing costs when the buyer is getting a loan than when they are paying cash.

5. Contingencies:

A contingency is an additional provision added to a contract that grants the right to withdraw from the agreement under specific circumstances without incurring any penalties. Contingencies are commonly utilized by buyers who may not be completely certain or prepared to proceed with the purchase of a property, allowing them extra time to organize their affairs.

When submitting an offer, it is important to decide whether to include a contingency and, if so, to determine its specific conditions. Real estate contracts often incorporate several standard contingencies that can be utilized. Here are some of the most prevalent ones:

Inspection Contingency:

Referred to as the "Due Diligence Period" or "Due Diligence Contingency," this provision grants the buyer a specified timeframe, usually between 5 and 10 days, to perform necessary evaluations and assessments to ensure their decision to purchase the property. This may involve inspections, appraisals, or contractor evaluations.

If, at any point during the inspection period, the buyer chooses to withdraw from the deal for any reason, they have the freedom to do so. This contingency is particularly useful for buyers who lack expertise in property inspections or estimating repair costs. The buyer can take advantage of this period to conduct a thorough property inspection and obtain contractor estimates for any required work. In the event of unforeseen issues, the buyer can request a discount or repairs or alternatively, choose to back out of the agreement.

Financing Contingency:

One of the most commonly used contingencies, the financing contingency, states that the buyer's offer is contingent upon securing appropriate financing for the property. It typically specifies the type of financing (e.g., FHA loan, conventional loan), the terms (e.g., interest rate, down payment), and the timeframe.

For example, a typical financing contingency may read as follows:

"Buyer shall have 20 days from the date of a binding agreement (the 'financing contingency period') to determine if the buyer can obtain a loan with the following terms:

- Loan Amount: 96.5% of the total purchase price of the property
- Term: 30 years

- Interest Rate: No higher than 5.25%
- Loan Type: FHA (Federal Housing Administration)

This agreement shall be terminated without penalty to the buyer if the buyer is unable to obtain the loan described above and notifies the seller in writing within the financing contingency period."

Including a financing, contingency is advisable for any buyer intending to use financing for their property purchase. In the worst-case scenario of financing falling through, the buyer retains the option to withdraw from the agreement without incurring any penalties.

Appraisal Contingency:

This contingency offers two options:

If an appraisal cannot be obtained for the property at a value equal to or higher than the purchase price, the buyer can choose to back out of the deal.

If an appraisal cannot be obtained for the property at a value equal to or higher than the purchase price, the buyer can request that the seller lower the price. If the seller refuses, the buyer has the right to back out of the deal.

The appraisal contingency is often tied to the financing contingency, as lenders typically do not finance a loan above the appraised value of the property.

Selling A Current Property:

This particular contingency has gained popularity among homeowners who are looking to upgrade their current house. It grants the buyer the right to withdraw from the deal if they are unable to sell her existing residence to another buyer. Typically, the contingency specifies a specific period during which the contract remains in effect, allowing the buyer sufficient time to sell their other property.

While investors generally do not utilize this contingency, it is commonly employed by homeowners who are transitioning from one house to another.

Although there are numerous other possible contingencies that may be found or used in real estate contracts, the ones mentioned above are the most prevalent, serving as the foundation for many others.

Additional contingencies that you may encounter in the future include:

- Termite Letter Contingency
- Lead Paint Test Contingency
- Deed Contingency (specifying the expected type of deed from the seller at closing)
- Radon Testing Contingency
- Mold Inspection Contingency
- Sewer Inspection Contingency
- Private Well Inspection Contingency
- Home Owner Association Documents Contingency
- Insurance Contingency (ensuring the acquisition of insurance at a reasonable price)

Rules for Using Contingencies

Rule #1: Minimizing the number of contingencies in your offer increases its appeal to the seller.

While this principle may seem self-evident, it's worth examining it from the seller's standpoint. The seller's objective is to sell their property swiftly and smoothly, and each contingency included in your offer represents a potential opportunity for you to withdraw from the agreement prior to its completion.

As a result, it's in your best interest as a buyer to put as few contingencies in place as possible. Someone isn't trying to imply that you should never utilize a backup plan since they may be crucial in some situations, but you should only rely on them if possible. Furthermore, if you can offer without stipulations, it will be considerably more attractive than the alternatives.

Naturally, you take a risk by only including a contingency in your offer if you have had the property examined (or have done it yourself) and are pretty sure that you want to continue ahead.

Rule #2: Limit your offer to a single contingency.

Maybe you already knew that; perhaps you didn't. Consider it from the seller's stance:

They would want a swift and orderly sale of their property; therefore, if you include any preconditions in your offer, they may have to reject it.

Although it may seem more comforting to include several contingencies in your offer—after all, this gives you more room to back out, right?—in reality, a single contingency is typically enough protection. The inspection contingency is the sole contingency for 80% of an offer (the remaining 20% have no contingencies).

The inspection contingency will allow you a certain amount of time to make sure you want to and can purchase the property; often, this is anything from 5 to 10 days. During this time, you will order the property inspection, get the finance squared up, draft the scope of work, have contractors come out to the property to give bids, contact the insurance agent for quotations, and so on.

TIP: Technically, you may use an inspection or due diligence contingency to get out of an agreement if there is a problem with the inspection, but in practice, you can use it to get out of a deal for any reason. In the worst case, if the seller asks you why you are backing out, you may always state that your contractor bids came in higher than anticipated and that your numbers don't work. The underlying reason you're backing out has nothing to do with inspections or contractors.

By the time the inspection period is up, you will be very confident about whether you are ready to proceed with this property. If you have found anything alarming (structure difficulties, mold, neglected repair bills, etc.), you could go back to the seller to negotiate a lower price, and in worst-case scenario, you might pull out of the agreement.

Rule #3: Only execute a contingency if necessary.

Many investors employ the strategy of submitting numerous offers, each with contingencies, and only delve into property details if their offer is accepted. While this approach allows for the quick submission of multiple offers, it also increases the likelihood of backing out of one or more deals utilizing contingencies.

There may be instances where you discover more extensive repair work than anticipated, encounter costly structural issues, or determine that the property's layout could pose challenges for resale. In such cases, exercising caution may lead to backing out of deals.

However, it's important to be mindful of the potential consequences of frequently backing out of deals. Developing a reputation for using contingencies to withdraw from contracts can negatively impact your reputation. This is especially true when repeatedly working with the same listing agents, such as when purchasing REO properties. Sellers are primarily interested in expeditiously and efficiently disposing of their properties. If they perceive that you are prone to wasting their time by frequently backing out of deals, they may be disinclined to accept your offers.

If you find yourself needing to utilize contingencies, it's worth considering alternative strategies or approaches to mitigate potential repercussions.

Rule #4: Contingencies can be negotiating tools.

You don't necessarily have to utilize your contingency to back out of a deal just because it's not working out in your favor. Instead, you can leverage that contingency as an opportunity to reopen negotiations with the seller.

For instance, let's consider a scenario where you discover significant plumbing issues during the inspection, which would require an additional $3000 in plumbing work. Instead of immediately using your contingency to withdraw from the deal, you can use it as a chance to request the seller lower the price by $3000. By doing so, you keep the deal intact and highlight that the seller might encounter the same issue with the next potential buyer, effectively passing on the cost of plumbing repairs to them.

Similarly, if your financing falls through, rather than immediately utilizing the contingency to exit the deal, you could explore the possibility of reopening negotiations, particularly regarding seller financing, especially if the seller is a bank.

The crucial point to remember is that even when you exercise a contingency, it doesn't have to be solely for backing out of the deal. Instead, it can be employed to revisit the original agreement and seek a reasonable compromise to resolve the underlying issue(s) and satisfy both parties involved.

Negotiating Tips

Dealing directly with private sellers sometimes means negotiating over the phone or in person. However, be cautious against making initial proposals or entering into negotiations over the phone when you're still learning the ropes, and it's good to be ready just in case.

There could be a whole book written on the subject of bargaining (and there are many excellent books on the topic that you should consider reading), the following are some of the most crucial principles you should practice right now.

Tip #1: Let the Other Party Speak First

People often say, "Never make the first offer...let the other party do it." This is excellent advice, but do you know why that will help your negotiating position?

There are two reasons:

1. Firstly, stating your position first allows you to establish a midpoint in the negotiation. Inexperienced negotiators often find themselves compromising and settling around the midpoint. For instance, if one negotiator starts with an asking price of $200 and the other begins with an offer of $100, the negotiation typically ends around $150—the midpoint. This tendency arises from the natural inclination not to give more or less than one receives, leading parties to adjust their offers by a similar amount as the other party.

However, when the other party presents their position first, you have the opportunity to redefine the negotiation's midpoint. In the given example, if the seller states their asking price as $200, the buyer can counter with an offer of $60, effectively shifting the midpoint of the negotiation to $130. Conversely, if the buyer opens the negotiation with an offer of $100, the seller can increase their asking price to $260, thereby raising the midpoint to $180. This demonstrates that the party making the first move is at a disadvantage compared to the party who waits, as the latter can shape and define the midpoint to their advantage.

2. Secondly, there is a possibility that the other party's initial offer may be more favorable than the first offer you would have made. Let's consider a situation where you need to hire a plumber, and your budget for a specific project is $500. If you were to disclose upfront that you have a bud-

get of $500 (hoping that the plumber wouldn't ask for more), what if the plumber had initially planned to charge only $300? By revealing your budget first, you have provided the plumber with information about your maximum spending capacity, giving them little reason to quote anything less. By disclosing your position prematurely, you inadvertently relinquish valuable information to the other party, allowing them to exploit it to extract the highest possible amount from you.

Tip #2: Stop Talking and Start Listening

One of the most powerful negotiation techniques is to refrain from speaking and instead focus on listening. Although it can be challenging, allowing for moments of silence during negotiations can yield significant benefits. Just remember that if you feel uncomfortable, the person you're negotiating with likely feels the same way. In these uncomfortable situations, one party often concedes to break the awkward silence.

Next time you find yourself negotiating and the other party presents an offer, make a conscious effort to remain silent. Whether it's for a few seconds or several minutes, let the other person break the silence. You'll be surprised to discover that they often interpret your silence as dissatisfaction or frustration, prompting them to revise their offer or make concessions. Skilled negotiators utilize this tactic to elicit progressively lower offers from less-experienced counterparts without needing to make counteroffers themselves.

This simple yet valuable negotiation tactic can become one of your most useful tools.

Tip #3: Information is Power

In approximately 95% of negotiations involving seasoned negotiators, the party with the most information tends to achieve a better outcome. When negotiating, it's crucial to gather as much information as possible, not only about the subject of the negotiation but also about the other party and their motivations.

While many people assume that negotiations primarily revolve around monetary factors, this isn't always the case. Astute negotiators recognize that solving a problem can hold greater significance than offering the highest amount of money.

For example, consider a scenario where two buyers express interest in a property at an open house. The first buyer assumes that the seller seeks the highest possible price and offers the full asking price, but it takes two months to close the deal due to financing and inspection processes. The second buyer engages in conversation with the seller to understand their motivations. The seller reveals that they have received a job offer in another state and need to move within the next two weeks. The second buyer presents an offer of $10,000 less than the asking price but agrees to close the deal within two weeks without any financing or inspection contingencies. Despite offering a lower price, the second buyer likely addresses a problem that holds greater importance to the seller, which outweighs the price difference. Gathering the seller's information before making an offer can lead to more favorable negotiation outcomes.

Tip #4: Check Your Ego at the Door

Recall the last time you negotiated with a charming person. Now, think about an encounter with an arrogant individual. Which one made you more inclined to gain an advantage?

Often, we assume that the other party in a negotiation seeks tangible gains, such as more money or better terms. However, many individuals who pride themselves on their negotiating skills are more interested in satisfying their egos than achieving tangible outcomes. While some individuals prioritize obtaining every extra penny in a deal, others are willing to accept a discounted price (as long as it surpasses their minimum threshold) in exchange for ego-stroking.

In real estate negotiations, this could involve praising a contractor for their highly recommended work or highlighting an investor/buyer's exceptional ability to execute cost-effective renovations. It might even entail playfully confessing to a wholesaler how challenging it is to negotiate with them due to their expertise. You'd be surprised how much genuine flattery can significantly influence negotiation outcomes. Not only does it encourage the other party to lower their defenses, but it also creates a sense of obligation to reciprocate the favor in some way. Make sure to provide them with an opportunity to do so immediately, whether in the form of a lower price or any other desired outcome.

4.2 Real Estate Contract Law

Real estate contracts are the formal deals that control the buying, selling, and financing of property, as well as how the real estate agent business works. There are many different kinds of contracts in this group, such as deals to sell or rent a property, choice contracts, mortgage contracts, loan agreements, listing contracts, and marketing contracts. Each type sets up different parts of real estate deals and client ties, as well as the compensations that go with them.

When working with real estate contracts, it's important to understand the basic ideas that apply to all contracts. These ideas give you a strong foundation for understanding the details of different kinds of contracts.

A contract is an agreement between two or more people who have come to an understanding, or "meeting of the minds," to do or not do certain things. The law says that for a deal to be legally binding, it must meet certain criteria. Parties can't count on the courts to enforce contract terms if they don't meet these requirements correctly.

It's important to remember that a contract is not a common form or a set of words on a piece of paper. Instead, it includes the unwritten deal that was made during the "meeting of the minds" between the two groups. A court can look at the legal state of a contract in one of these four ways to decide if it is valid and enforceable:

Valid: A valid contract meets all of the legal requirements for being valid. If a deal is written down, it can be enforced within a certain amount of time. In the same way, a legal informal agreement can usually be enforced within a certain amount of time, but there are some exceptions that will be explained below.

Valid but unenforceable: Some state rules say that in order for a contract to be valid, it must be in writing. These rules are especially important when it comes to the transfer of property rights. So, a verbal deal may meet the standards for being legal, but the parties cannot go to court to make it happen. Long-term silent leases and real estate sales contracts made over the phone are examples of contracts that are legal but can't be enforced.

Even though these contracts can't be enforced, it's important to note that they are still legal. If both sides follow the deal to the letter, the result may not change.

Void: A void contract doesn't meet the requirements for being legal, so it's not even a contract. An empty contract can't be used by either party. For example, a contract is not valid if there is no thought or if it is used to try to get money from a business. People also say that these contracts are "null and void."

Voidable: A voidable contract seems legal at first, but a party who did something wrong can get out of it. Only the person who says they are disabled has the right to get out of the deal. For example, a party may choose to back out of a contract if they can show that it was made under pressure, coercion, or fraud. To be legal, the decision to back out must be made within a certain amount of time. If, on the other hand, the person who has the right to back out of the contract chooses to keep it, the contract goes from being voidable to being legal.

A deal that can be broken is different from one that can't be broken at all, which is what makes the difference between the two.

4.3. Contract Creation

Offer and acceptance:

The process of making an offer and having it accepted is very important for making a legal contract. The offeror gives the offeree the terms of the contract in the form of an offer. A contract is made when the offeree accepts all of the terms without making any changes. When the person accepting the offer tells the person making the offer, the offer turns into a legally binding contract.

Offer:

An offer shows that the person making it wants to make a deal with the person receiving it. Both parties agree to do certain things in exchange for the other party doing those things. In contracts to buy or rent real estate, the offer must be made in writing and include all of the terms of the deal. If the deal has an end date and the phrase "time is of the essence," it ends at the exact time it says it does. If there isn't a set amount of time, the person being offered has a fair amount of time to accept.

Acceptance:

Acceptance gives the person who gets the deal the power to accept it. For acceptance to be valid, the person receiving the offer must accept all of the terms in a clear and straightforward way and sign the offer, ideally with a date. The offeror must then be told that the offer has been accepted. If acceptance is sent through the mail, it is valid as soon as it is put in the mail.

Counteroffer:

The offeree makes a counteroffer when they change the terms of the offer, which makes the original offer null and useless. At this point, the offeree becomes the offeror, and the right to accept the counteroffer passes to a new offeree. If the counteroffer is accepted, it becomes a legal contract as long as all the other conditions are met.

For example, if a seller changes the end date of a buyer's offer by one day, signs it, and sends it back to the buyer, the buyer's original offer is no longer valid, and any earlier agreement is no longer binding. The buyer can accept the seller's new offer, which is now called a counteroffer. If the buyer agrees to the counteroffer, it turns into a legally binding contract.

Offer revocation:

Offers can be taken back by the person who made them before the person to whom they were made can say yes. When an offer is revoked, both the offer and the offeree's right to accept it are gone.

For example, if a buyer makes an offer to buy a house at the stated price but then has to change their plans because a family member dies, they can call the seller right away and tell them they no longer want the house. Since the seller hasn't told the buyer that they've accepted the offer yet, the offer is officially over.

If the offeree pays something to keep the offer open and the offeror takes it, a choice is made that makes it impossible for the offeror to pull the offer during the time period stated.

Offer termination:

An offer can end in a number of ways, including acceptance (which makes it a contract), refusal, withdrawal by the offeror, the passing of time (expiration), a counteroffer, or the death or illness of one of the parties.

Contract Assignment:

A real estate contract that is not for personal services can be given to someone else unless the deal says that it can't be. Listing agreements are not transferable because they are personal service contracts between agents and their clients. But sales contracts can be given to someone else because they are for the purchase of real property and not for personal services. This is usually used in wholesaling.

Contract preparation:

State rules set limits on how much real estate brokers and managers can be involved in putting together real estate contracts. These rules, which are often called "broker-lawyer accords," say how much brokers and agents can do and what kinds of contracts they can handle. Depending on the state, dealers and managers are sometimes not allowed to write contracts on their own. But they can use standard forms and fill in the details they need on those forms.

When a broker or agent agrees to finish real estate contracts, they are usually practicing law without a license, unless they are a party to the contract, like a sale agreement or sales contract. Brokers and managers may need to finish leases, mortgages, contracts for deeds, or promissory notes that they have nothing to do with.

When writing and reading contracts on behalf of their clients, agents need to know exactly what they can and cannot do. If brokers don't follow the law, they are not only practicing law without the right license, but customers who depend on the contract's validity could file a case against them. It is important for agents to know their legal rights and limits so they can protect themselves and help their clients with contracts in a reliable way.

4.4. Classifications Of Contracts

Written vs. verbal:

A contract might be an oral agreement or a written arrangement. Even though they include commitments, some oral agreements are legitimate and binding while others could not be. For instance, in many jurisdictions, in order to be enforceable, listing agreements, sales contracts, and leases longer than one year must be in writing.

Inferred vs. Express:

An express contract is one in which the terms and conditions have been clearly expressed and accepted by all parties, either orally or in writing. However, an implicit contract is one that may be deduced from the behavior of the parties involved and is an unwritten or inadvertent agreement. An instance of an implied contract is implied agency, in which an agent works on behalf of a buyer by negotiating a price lower than the listed price without a formal contract. In particular, if the agent receives payment for their services, this unintended conduct may result in the establishment of an implicit contract with the customer.

Bilateral vs. Unilateral Contracts:

In a unilateral contract, one party promises something in return for the other party doing a specific act. The later party is not required to do anything, but if they do, the first party must keep their word. An example of a unilateral contract is an option contract, in which the party providing the option guarantees to sell a property if the potential buyer decides to exercise the option. The owner must sell if the option is exercised, even if the prospective buyer is not required to buy.

Contrarily, a bilateral contract is a pact in which both parties agree to carry out their own responsibilities in return for the other party's performance. An exclusive listing is an example of a bilateral agreement where the seller agrees to pay the broker upon the sale of the property and the broker agrees to market the property assiduously.

Execution vs. Executory:

A contract is considered complete and executed when neither party is left with any unfinished business. An inked lease agreement that has expired or been finished, for instance, allows the landlord to retake ownership of the property and releases the tenant from rent obligations.

Contrarily, an executory contract is one whose performance has not yet been fully carried out. An executory contract is one in which the parties have agreed to purchase and sell, but payment has not yet been made by the buyer, and the seller has not yet transferred ownership of the property via a deed.

4.5. Forms of Contract Termination

A contract may be terminated, often referred to as canceled or discharged, for a number of reasons. Here are a few reasons a contract could be terminated:

Performance:

A contract expires whenever all parties have fulfilled their commitments. Additionally, if both parties agree, it may be ended by incomplete performance. In rare circumstances, even if not all of the terms of the contract have been completely complied with, adequate performance as determined by a court may be sufficient.

Infeasibility:

Though a contract becomes difficult to carry out, it may be terminated even though it is otherwise legitimate. Contracts involving certain personal services, for instance, depend on a person's special skills that cannot be duplicated by another person. The contract may be terminated in the event of such a person's death or material disability.

Mutual Agreement:

The contract may be canceled or renounced if both parties agree to do so. They must satisfy the conditions for the new agreement's legitimacy if they want to replace the canceled one with it. The term "novation" refers to this procedure.

Cooling-Period Rescission: The act of voiding a contract is known as rescinding it. A statutory "cooling-off period" after the parties enter into the contract is permitted under specific agreements in several jurisdictions. The parties may terminate the agreement within this time without giving a reason, and the party exercising the cancellation is not responsible for any failure to fulfill it. For example, a customer who buys a property in a brand-new resort development may only have a small window of time to second-guess their choice without feeling pressured by obstinate sales methods.

Revocation: Revocation is the act of one party terminating the agreement without the approval of the other party. While all parties have the ability to revoke, they may not always have a valid reason to do so. For instance, a seller may revoke a listing to remove a property from the market. A revocation may not release a party from a contract's duties unless there are good reasons for doing so. For instance, a seller who cancels a listing without a valid reason may be required to pay a fee if the broker locates a buyer or to cover the broker's marketing costs if none exist.

Abandonment: Abandonment occurs when parties break their contractual commitments. The parties may be able to terminate the contract in such circumstances.

Time Expiration: If a contract has an end date, it automatically expires when that time has passed.

Contract Nullity: If a contract is null, it may be terminated without a formal disaffirmation. A voidable contract may be revoked or terminated by operation of law.

4.6. Breach of contract

A breach of contract occurs when the terms of a deal are not kept. It is also called "default," and it gives the damaged party the right to go to court.

The damaged party can use the following court options:

Rescission: If one party is damaged by the contract, they can choose to withdraw it. This cancels the deal and puts both parties back where they were before the contract. This includes giving back any money that was traded.

Loss: A loss means that the person who broke the contract has to give up something that was in the contract. For example, if a buyer breaks a sales deal, they may have to give up their earnest money deposit.

Damages Suit: The damaged party has the right to go to civil court and file a case to get money for the harm done. The statute of limitations sets a time limit for starting a case, and it's important to do so. If the contract says that you have to pay a certain amount if you break it, this is called "liquidated damages." If there is no such clause, the damaged party can sue for unliquidated losses, and the court will decide how much is fair.

Suit for Specific Performance: A suit for specific performance is meant to force the party who broke the contract to live up to its terms. This type of legal action is often taken when it is hard to figure out how much damage was done because the real property in question is unique. For example, if a sale or lease contract is broken, the buyer or seller can ask the court to force the party who broke the contract to finish the deal, even if the party who broke the contract would rather pay a monetary settlement.

4.7. Determining The Value of the Subject Property:

There are financial costs to take into consideration when assessing a house's value.

Many newer investors will see the tax assessment for a property and assume that the property's assessed value is in some way indicative of the property's value. This is different.

While the assessed value of a property could end up being close to the actual value of the property, it is more likely to be a coincidence than anything else.

There are a few reasons for this:

- Local assessments are done infrequently. It's possible that the last time a review was done, the housing market was very different and values were far from where they are now (in either direction).
- The city or county often doesn't have the best data on property characteristics. For example, a property may have originally been intended to be a three-bedroom, two-bath property. Still, due to changes in the planning or work done by previous owners, it could now be a four-bedroom, three-bath property. If the proper per-

mits weren't pulled (or even if they weren't recorded correctly), the local government wouldn't know about the change, and no new assessment would be triggered.

- Local assessors don't enter the property, so they have no idea what the inside looks like. From the outside, two condos may look identical. Still, inside, one might have granite, hardwood, upgraded fixtures, a Jacuzzi tub, and $15,000 worth of upgraded appliances, while the other might use all builder-grade materials.
- Local assessments can be off by 30% or more (in either direction). So be careful and don't rely only on the tax assessment to help you determine a property's value.

4.8. Calculating Fixed Costs:

Fixed costs encompass a variety of fees, commissions, and expenses related to investment projects, excluding the actual rehabilitation costs. Although these costs vary depending on the investor and project location, they can be grouped into three main categories:

1. Purchase Costs:

These costs are associated with acquiring a property and can be further divided as follows:

a) Inspection Costs:

Prior to purchasing a property, a thorough inspection is conducted by a reliable inspector. Typically, the cost of a comprehensive property inspection is around $400.

b) Closing Costs:

When finalizing a property purchase, there are standard closing costs that the buyer is responsible for. These costs typically include expenses such as recording fees, title searches, courier fees, state taxes, document review fees, attorney fees, and more. The closing attorney takes these costs into account to make sure the title is clear and the new deed is recorded correctly. On average, these closing costs amount to approximately $1000, although they can vary depending on the location and the type of purchase (e.g., REO purchase).

c) Lender Fees:

For financing property acquisitions, investors often rely on the same lender who charges upfront fees to cover the loan. These fees may include, credit report fee, underwriting fee, document preparation fee, processing fee, appraisal fee, a loan origination fee, flood certification fee and other charges. While the specific costs depend on the investor, lender, and property purchase price, the average total for these lender fees is around $2000 depending on the location, per property in a typical acquisition.

2. Holding Costs:

Holding costs encompass the expenses incurred between the property's acquisition and its eventual sale. For example purposes only, these costs can be further broken down as follows:

a) Mortgage Payments:

The average duration of a project, which typically lasts 4-6 months, the monthly mortgage payment for the property amounts to approximately $500. Thus, a total of approximately $2500 is paid to the lender to maintain the property during this period.

b) Property Taxes:

Purchased properties incur an annual property tax of around $1400. Therefore, if the property is held for 4-6 months, the average property tax expense per project amounts to roughly $600.

c) Utilities:

To facilitate the work of contractors and promptly address any property issues, utilities such as electricity, water, and gas need to remain active throughout the rehabilitation process. Incorporating other expenses, utility expenses for properties typically reach around $200 per month over the duration of the project. Thus, the average utility costs amount to approximately $1000 per project, lasting 4-6 months.

d) Insurance:

Insurance costs for properties typically range from $350 to $400 per year. As a result, an allocation of around $200 is made to cover insurance expenses for each project.

3. Selling Costs:

When you sell a house, you have to pay fees and profits, which are part of the selling costs. Different buyers may use different ways to promote their projects, but the prices of selling can be further broken down as follows:

Commissions:

Half of fees can be saved if you partner with a real estate agent/broker. However, if the buyer has their own agent, which is often the case, you must pay them around 3% of the sale price of the home. If a property sells for about $120,000, thus the buyer's realtor will charge roughly $3600. The additional fees that must be paid to your broker raises the total costs for each property transaction to, on average, $3,600.

Closing expenses: In some markets, buyers often request that sellers cover all or a portion of their closing expenses. Using the previous examples there would be an average of $3,600 - $4,000 in closing fees for the buyer during a buyer's market.

Home warranty: The majority of first-time homebuyers want a home warranty from the seller as a condition of the transaction. This will raise the price of selling by around $500.

Termite Letter: Many purchasers and their lenders will want you to provide evidence of a termite inspection at the time of sale in addition to the house warranty. Typically, this costs a little around $100.

MLS Fees: Your agent has the responsibility of covering the cost of listing the home on the local MLS. The typical cost of this is $100, which may be covered by your agent.

As was previously said, purchasing, owning, and selling real estate are all associated with a number of fixed expenses and fees.

4.9. Your Profit

At some point, you will have to determine the minimum amount of profit you are willing to work for on a particular rehab. Several factors often determine this:

- **Price Point:** Most investors understand that rehabbing and reselling a $100K house will likely generate less profit than rehabbing and reselling a $500K home. Because the amount of cash required to do these types of deals and the risks involved are more substantial, the profits also tend to be more significant. While many investors might be happy with a $15K profit on a $100K resale, these same investors might require a $50K profit on a $500K resale.
- **Experience:** New investors are likely to settle for smaller profits than more experienced investors. A $5K profit might sound like a massive accomplishment for investors doing their first deal. But, once these investors realize the amount of time and energy involved in flipping a house, they likely want to avoid settling for such small gains.
- **Amount of Risk:** Projects that incur greater risk should also have the opportunity for greater reward. While an investor may be happy with a small profit on a condo that only required new paint and carpet, that same investor will want to see the possibility of much greater earnings if there is a risky foundation or waterproofing work needed. Because these significant repairs run the

risk of budget and schedule overruns, extra profit should be built-in to compensate for those risks.

- **Amount of Time:** Most investors will demand higher returns for projects that take several months than those that only take a few weeks. Not only does the extra time decrease the overall rate of return, but the investor will likely have to invest a much larger number of hours, so higher profits will be needed to maintain an hourly wage.
- **Estimating Rehab Costs:** The most common question investors ask is, "How do I accurately estimate rehab costs for a flip project?" Unfortunately, the answer to this question is complex. For more investors, it is the biggest roadblock standing in the way of them feeling ready to invest. While there is no magic bullet to estimating rehab costs, there are several options at your disposal, such as www.rehabvaluator.com. The one thing that is promised is that the more rehabs you do, the easier it will get.

Remember that before determining renovation costs, you will need to inspect and assemble a "scope of work," which is a list of renovation items you plan to complete during the rehab.

4.10. Finding Properties

Discovering real estate opportunities can be approached in various ways, each with its own enthusiasts. Seasoned real estate investors often dedicate years to honing their skills in a specific method of attracting sales, relying exclusively on that approach to nurture and expand their businesses. Unfortunately, this strategy of solely relying on a single marketing technique can have severe repercussions if that primary source of deals slows down or disappears altogether.

The MLS

The Multiple Listing Service (MLS), commonly known as the MLS, serves as a centralized platform where listing agents (real estate agents representing sellers) typically advertise their properties for sale. Simultaneously, selling agents (real estate agents representing buyers, also referred to as "buyer's agents") search for suitable properties on behalf of their clients.

Contrary to popular belief, there is no universal MLS encompassing the entire nation. Instead, most major cities have their own MLS, and some cities even boast multiple listing services. Any property available for sale through a real estate agent, including retail sales, REOs, and a majority of short sales, will be listed on the MLS.

Markets undergo rapid transformations, and relying solely on one avenue to acquire properties can lead to financial setbacks and a bleak outlook for future opportunities. While utilizing the MLS for certain deals is advisable, it is crucial not to invest all your resources and efforts solely in that particular channel.

Benefits of Using the MLS for Deal Flow

There are lots of benefits to focusing on the MLS for your deals. First and foremost, using the MLS requires very little, if any, marketing effort. A considerable percentage of distressed property sales are listed right on the MLS, meaning the deals come to you instead of you having to market for them. This can save you a lot of money on marketing costs and time on other marketing efforts.

Second, if you rely on real estate agents to bring you MLS deals (or to provide you with an automated feed of MLS deals), there is no cost to using the MLS.

Third, if you're investing in distressed properties, there are many resources for finding available properties better than the MLS. Local real estate agents will list nearly all the REOs sold by central banks. Those agents will almost always publicly market their REOs through their local MLS; likewise, most short sales are sold directly through the MLS.

Drawbacks of Using the MLS for Deal Flow

The biggest drawback of using the MLS for deals is that everyone uses it because it's easy and generally accessible. Competition for sales on the MLS is often fierce, with some properties attracting dozens of offers from investors and homeowners alike. And because you're going to be more conservative (i.e., more successful) than many of your fellow investors, you're probably not offering as much as they are for the same properties. This means that you're going to make a lot of offers but end up with very few deals.

Many deals that hit the MLS are already sold before being listed! Listing agents will sometimes pass the best deals to their favorite investors, who lock the deal up before it officially gets listed for sale and then put it on the MLS to make it look like the agent was doing the right thing. Likewise, with short sales, most lenders require that short sales be listed on the MLS before they will consider taking a reduced payoff, but often, listing agents are only listing the properties on the MLS to satisfy this condition; in many cases, the property was already under contract well before the agent put it on the MLS for sale.

The biggest downside to relying on the MLS for deals is that getting access to the MLS can be difficult. In most states, you need to be a licensed real estate agent to gain direct access to all the MLS data. If you're not approved, some websites will provide you with much of the same data as the MLS (www.realtor.com is a great example). Still, these sites will offer only some of the most critical information, such as the confidential agent remarks and lockbox codes to get you into the property. Likewise, when you find a real estate agent to work with, they will likely be able to automatically email you listings that match your buying criteria as they become available on the MLS. Still, again, you will get only some of the essential data this way.

If you decide to focus on the MLS for deal flow, it is highly recommended that you consider getting your real estate license. It's a significant time commitment to get the right one and will require a reasonable investment, but any serious investor who wants to buy off the MLS should have direct access.

Deciphering MLS Listings

If you're using the MLS as a source of deals, you will need to get good at deciphering which MLS listings are distressed properties and which are retail properties. Sometimes the listing agent will make it very easy to tell, for example, they may put "BANK OWNED FORECLOSURE!" in the comments.

But, other times, it's a lot more challenging to determine a property's status. And, even if you can tell which properties are distressed by looking through the listings, that still requires you to look through EVERY new listing to see which are potential deals and which are not.

Experienced investors have learned that there are several ways you can filter distressed listings on the MLS without having to look through every listing one by one (and if you choose to look through each listing, this will give you an idea of what to look for). To provide some examples of how to filter, use an advanced search across all listings, looking for the following words and phrases:

To indicate that the property is likely an REO:

- "Sold as-is."
- "Foreclosure."

- "No disclosure from the seller."
- "Lender Owned."
- "Call agent for the lockbox code."
- "Must Pre-Qual w/Preferred Lender."
- "Pre-qual or proof of funds required with all offers."
- "Corporate owner."

To indicate that the property is a short sale:

- "Potential short sale."
- "Lender approval required."
- "Pending lender approval."

To indicate that the property is generally distressed (whether an REO, short sale or private sale):

- "Handyman Special."
- "Fixer Upper."
- "Cash only."
- "Will not qualify for FHA financing."
- "Needs some TLC."

Online/Auctions:

Over the past several years, marketing and selling online have become a massive outlet for distressed property sales. You can find house sales on websites run by everyone from the U.S. government to large auction houses to mom-and-pop wholesalers looking to move a property now and again. While it is impossible to cover all the different online property sale websites, here is an overview of some of the most popular outlets. They are discussed with the types of properties they sell to help you decide why you might (or might not) want to consider looking for houses online.

HUD Properties (HudHomeStore.com)

The U.S. government's Department of Housing and Urban Development (HUD) runs the most significant operation for selling houses online. To give some background, if a homeowner buys a house using an FHA loan and later gets foreclosed upon, the foreclosed home reverts to ownership by HUD. HUD then sells these foreclosed houses online to owner-occupants, investors, non-profit organizations, etc. Because HUD has so many homes in its inventory, many investors will build their entire strategy around buying HUD foreclosures.

The HUD website is http://www.hudhomestore.com, and anyone can browse the site to see what properties are listed in a given area. To bid on a HUD house, you must work with a real estate agent registered with HUD to place bids; most buyers' agents can do this. When first listed for public bidding, HUD properties are targeted at owner-occupants, and investors cannot bid on them. But if a property doesn't sell to an owner-occupant within a specified period (5 or 30 days, depending on property condition), it is open to investors for bidding.

Houses in good condition often sell to owner-occupants without investors ever getting to bid. Still, those houses are in more distressed condition or in areas where HUD has more inventory than buyers will often become available to investors. The way the bidding works is that HUD will take all the offers submitted the previous day and review them each day. They will rank the recommendations based on how much money HUD will net on the sale, and if the offer that earns them the highest amount meets their minimum acceptable amount, that offer will be accepted.

Unlike other foreclosure or REO sales, the seller (in this case, HUD) doesn't care about any terms, conditions, or stipulations other than the net amount of money they receive on the sale. Therefore, there is no preference for owner-occupants versus investors or cash buyers versus financed buyers, it's a level playing field, and the highest offer wins. If none of the submissions provide a net amount to HUD that meets their minimum requirement, the house stays listed, and HUD will repeat the offer review process every day until they get an acceptable offer. As a buyer, you can submit a new request as often as you like (either a different offer or the same one), and you may find that HUD will eventually accept your offer.

While it's not publicized anywhere, most investors believe that HUD is willing to accept a net amount about 15% below the list price. Therefore, if a HUD property is listed for $100,000, your best chance to get HUD to accept your bid is to ensure that the net amount they will receive on the offer is at least $85,000. Below that amount, they will likely reject the bid and leave the property listed. That said, if a HUD property has been listed for a long time, HUD will often reduce the listing price and start considering bids lower (sometimes much lower) than 15% off the list price.

With HUD properties, investor buyers do not have an inspection period. Once you submit your signed contract and earnest money (after your offer is accepted), you're committed to buying the property or losing your earnest money deposit—no exceptions. You generally have two days from your offer's acceptance until the contract and EMD (earnest money deposit) are due. If the HUD office is local, you, or your agent, can drop the package off in person at the office. However, if the office is not local, you'll have to overnight it the day before it's due.

With that said, here's a little trick: While you don't have an inspection period with HUD purchases, you can use the day or two between the time the offer is accepted and the time the completed package is due for quick inspections. If you decide not to proceed with the purchase, don't send in the contract or earnest money, and HUD will relist the property without penalty.

1. **Home Path & Home Steps**

Two of the most common REO properties are those sold by Fannie Mae and Freddie Mac, two quasi-government agencies that underwrite and insure much of the conventional lending in the United States. When a traditional loan gets foreclosed upon, the property will often revert to Fannie Mae or Freddie Mac to be sold off, often as an REO.

Both agencies sell their REO inventory through real estate agents (on the MLS). Still, they both list their inventory on their websites. Typically, they require agents to make offers through websites (www.homepath.com and www.homesteps.com).

One downside to Fannie and Freddie REOs is that they give preferential treatment to owner-occupants; most inventory is made available to investors 15 days after homeowners get the first opportunity to buy. However, if the 15 days go by without an accepted offer from a homeowner, the property is opened up for investor bidding, and it's often possible at this point to get some good deals. Because owner-occupants will generally buy the lovely houses in the first 15-day period, the places that open up to investors tend to need renovation more. Still, again, these are often the houses that also provide the most profit potential.

2. **Auction.com and Other REO Auction Sites**

The second primary classification of online property websites is "auction" sites. Some of the most popular sites in this category are Auction.com (www.auction.com),

Williams & Williams Auctions (www.williamsauction.com) and Hubzu (www.hubzu.com) are also at the top. These sites typically auction off REO properties that didn't sell through the standard REO channels (meaning they didn't sell when publicly listed on the MLS).

Generally, the auction takes place over several days or even weeks. If the bid reaches a certain amount, it may be accepted immediately, or the seller may choose to let the auction run its entire duration before determining the high bid. While some of these sites are auction sites, many are just "lead generation systems" for the sellers.

In an actual auction, the highest bidder will win. Sometimes the high bid may have to be above some minimum threshold (called the "reserve"), but assuming it's above the reserve and the buyer can pay, the sale is final once the bidding is complete. Unfortunately, this isn't the case with many of the so-called online auction sites. Instead, the highest bidder hasn't won anything, and the auction house will take the highest bid and submit it to the seller just like any other offer, waiting for the seller to decide if they want to take the offer, reject it, or make a counter-offer. Sometimes, bidders must wait weeks to find out if their high bid was accepted.

In addition, some of the sites will hold online and in-person auctions; Auction.com is known for going city to city and auctioning off extensive inventories of REO properties, some of which were previously available for purchase online and are only available in person. In some cases, for properties that don't sell the first time (in person or online) or where the seller doesn't accept the high bid, the properties are re-auctioned multiple times until sold.

While there is no rhyme or reason as to whether a seller will accept the high bid, generally speaking, sellers are looking for at least 65% of the property's value as it's listed (the auction house always lists what they believe the market value is). However, it often takes at least 80% to ensure the seller will seriously consider the offer.

Many investors find good deals using these auction sites, the process can be frustrating; if you're expecting a traditional auction experience, you will likely be disappointed.

3. **Classified Websites**

There are a few large, nationally recognized websites where private sellers can list and sell stuff they own. eBay (www.ebay.com) and Craigslist (www.craigslist.org) are among the largest. And many cities, especially the larger ones, will have their sites geared explicitly to local trade.

These sites are typically referred to as "classifieds" sites, as they are extensions of what used to happen in the classified sections of newspapers. While eBay isn't a traditional classifieds site, it does have some similarities, which is why it's lumped into this category.

On these sites, private sellers (homeowners and investors) often list real estate for sale. These are generally privately owned properties being sold as part of a traditional sale; in many cases, the owners may not be overly motivated, and the properties may not be distressed, so not every listing will be a potential deal. But there are enough distressed sellers and investors who sell on these sites and spend some time there looking for bargains.

4. **Wholesaling Websites**

The last major category of online property sites is those that allow investors to sell to other investors. This is typically called wholesaling, where one investor purchases or takes control of a property. Instead of improving the property and making a hefty profit, they would rather sell it to another investor to do the work and take a smaller profit.

While the idea is great in theory, in reality, most wholesalers could be better at pricing deals, so by the time they see a property and mark up the price to account for their profit, the property isn't much of a contract. In addition, because wholesaling is done in bulk, wholesalers are sometimes bad at estimating resale value and rehab costs, so any information they give you about a property should be thoroughly evaluated; do you due diligence.

But if you have a keen eye, there is no harm in looking, as most of these sites are free for buyers.

5. **Direct Marketing**

Direct marketing involves communicating directly with your potential customers (sellers, in this case). It can be done through many different means: the Internet, mail, over the phone, in person, etc. For this discussion, direct marketing is defined as one-on-one direct contact with your customer instead of blanket marketing and have customers contact you via advertising.

6. **Direct Mail**

Direct mail (D.M.) is still one of the most reliable forms of marketing for real estate deals. Because D.M. will allow you to target the broadest range of potential sellers quickly and at a reasonable cost, many real estate investors spend the bulk of their marketing time and money focused on D.M. leads.

Direct mail consists of creating postcards and letters that indicate your interest in buying property, sending them to a target audience of potential sellers, and then waiting for those sellers to contact you by phone, email or through your website. Your target audience of sellers could consist of distressed or retail owners, and your method of purchasing from different sellers may vary.

7. **Distressed Direct Mail Targets**

When targeting distressed sellers through D.M., you are more than likely going to be targeting homeowners who are underwater on their house; this means that the homeowner owes more than the home is worth, and the most common scenario for you to purchase that property would be through a short sale transaction.

When focusing a D.M. campaign on distressed owners, here are some of the most common groups of sellers to go after:

- Owners who are 30, 60, or 90 days late on their mortgages
- Owners who have been notified of a pending foreclosure
- Owners who have listed their house for sale on the MLS but the listings have expired

8. **Retail Direct Mail Targets**

While less common these days because fewer owners have house equity, it's still possible to find great retail deals through a well-created D.M. campaign. The nice thing about buying retail (meaning the homeowner is above water on their property and can sell without making a short sale) is that you won't need approval from the owner's lender, making the deal much faster and with much less hassle.

While retail D.M. campaigns can be targeted at homeowners, they are often targeted at other investors, such as landlords. This is because other savvy investors may have bought their properties long ago or for all cash and may have a lot of equity. Also, many landlords own property out-of-state, and managing those properties can get tiresome; many want to be independent of landlords. They will sell their properties at deep discounts if the right buyer comes along.

Here are the most common groups of retail sellers that direct marketers tend to go after:

- Absentee owners (generally landlords) who have owned their property for at least 7–10 years (meaning they likely have equity) or who purchased their property for cash
- Homeowners who have owned their properties for at least 7–10 years
- Blanket mailings to all houses within a subdivision, community, or geographic location

Creating Your Direct Mail Campaign

Putting together a direct mail campaign isn't rocket science but will take time and effort. Here are the basic steps that go into creating a D.M. campaign:

a. **Setting up your phone line and website for your D.M. leads:**

It is imperative to establish at least one reliable channel for prospective leads to get in touch with you. The two most common and effective ways are via phone or website. Most contact will be done via phone, and while you most certainly won't want to be giving out your cell phone number, there are plenty of options for getting a free or inexpensive phone number that you can use instead, e.g., Google Voice. You can set up a complimentary phone number (or several), have the number forwarded to a cell phone, and customize a voicemail message for when you don't answer. If you miss a call and receive a voicemail, Google Voice will transcribe the message and text it along with the calling number.

Set up a website to capture leads, as some people would prefer to check out a website before placing a phone call, and some want to wait to initiate a phone call. Your website should have all the essential information about who you are, what you do, and what the sales/purchase process is when dealing with you. It then allows the potential lead to contact you directly via a web form that goes to your email.

b. **Finding or generating your target mailing lists:**

Once you have your method(s) of contact set up to receive communication from potential leads, you will want to put together (or purchase) your list of references. There are many options for direct mail targets. While you can build your list by hand by sorting through public records and driving around town to find run-down properties, working with a list provider who can give you names for a reasonable price is best.

Many national companies can provide lists of absentee owners or 30-, 60-, or 90-day mortgage rates; in most markets, local companies can provide pre- and pending-foreclosure lists. For lists of expired MLS listings, you shouldn't have too much difficulty finding a local real estate agent who will work with you, especially if you're willing to pay a small fee or bring the agent in on the deal by allowing them to represent the seller in some way.

c. **Creating your marketing letter or card:**

The most crucial step in the process is to create the mailer you will send to prospects. Letters and postcards are the two most common types of mailers, and there is plenty of variety within those two groups. For example, some direct marketers prefer concise, vague handwritten notes on yellow paper ("yellow letters"), and others prefer page-long form-mail that details what the investor is looking for and proposing. Ultimately, there is no one correct answer, but below, some important things are discussed that you should consider when creating and tweaking your direct mail campaigns.

To give you an idea of the wide range of direct mailers you should be considering, and trying, are card samples and few letters. You can check two popular turnkey direct mail services www.YellowLetters.com and www.YellowLettersComplete.com as samples.

d. **Addressing, stuffing, stamping, and mailing your direct mail pieces:**

Once you have created your mailing list and mailer, it's time to assemble the package. For non-postcard mailings, you're going to need the following:

- Copies of your mailer: If you'll be handwriting, it's time to get to work. Other options are to print your mailer or to handwrite one and make color copies of the handwritten letter.

- Envelopes. Remember, one of the big keys to a successful direct mail campaign is to get as many prospects to open that envelope as possible. To achieve this, think about the types of envelopes you're more likely to open:
    - Handwritten Envelopes
    - Envelopes that aren't standard 4 x 9
    - Envelopes that are not white (especially pastel colors)
    - Envelopes that appear to contain an invitation
- Stamps: There are many options for stamping/sending your mailers. While bulk mail is more cost effective, the rate of delivery is slower. First-class stamps are preferred, despite the high price tag. It would help if you determined what works best for you based on your budget and goals. One trick here is to go to the post office and ask for decorative stamps instead of the standard first-class flag stamps; while they won't cost anything additional, it's just another way to get your mailer to appear personal, increasing the chances it will be opened.
- Return address labels: You'll want return address labels, as a high percentage of your mailers may get returned, especially if you're targeting homeowners near foreclosure and have already moved out of their homes. By getting the returned mail, you can remove these names from your list and save money on your follow-up mailings. It is recommended not to use your home address on the label but also not to use a P.O. Box address. Many UPS stores will provide mailboxes at a low cost that can be received using a street/suite address.

Advertising

Internet Marketing is simple: you create a website to capture leads and create online marketing campaigns to drive potential sellers to your site. However, while the concept of Internet marketing is simple, the real-life implementation can be anything but. There are many ways to drive traffic to your lead-capture site, some "organic" (meaning visitors get to your site via search engines or other cost-free mechanisms) and some paid.

Internet Marketing

Internet Marketing is simple: you create a website to capture leads and create online marketing campaigns to drive potential sellers to your site. However, while the concept of Internet Marketing is simple, the real-life implementation can be anything but. There are many ways to drive traffic to your lead-capture site, some "organic" (meaning visitors get to your site via search engines or other cost-free mechanisms) and some paid.

Organic Internet Traffic

The best way to drive organic traffic to your lead-capture site is to create a content-rich website that ranks high in the search engines for the types of Internet searches your potential sellers are doing. For example, let's say you want to buy distressed houses in Baltimore, MD. People who are interested in selling their distressed home in Baltimore may type the following into Google or another search engine:

"How can I sell my underwater home in Baltimore?"

When they type that or a similar phrase in a search engine, you'll want your website to show up at or near the top of the list. If the potential seller clicks on the link to your website, you can capture their information and generate a lead. Again, while it's easy in principle if you live in a larger or more popular geographic area, there are likely already many other investors with websites competing for these leads; you'll need to work hard to get your site ranked higher than theirs for the potential search traffic you're trying to get.

To get an idea of the competition you'll have for leads from organic search traffic, try this:

1. Point your Internet browser at one of the popular search engines (www.google.com, for example).
2. Do a search that is similar to what your potential targets might search for when looking to off-load their properties (for example, "sell my house quickly in Baltimore").
3. Look at how many results were returned for that search (in the example above, 35 million results were returned).

To be successful using this marketing route, you'll want your website to show up on (or very near) the first page, meaning the top 10 results. With 35 million competing pages, that will take time and some serious, dedicated effort.

Paid Internet Traffic

The alternative to getting free traffic to your website is paying for it. This is generally done by placing ads in various places on the Internet where your potential seller leads might see them. The most common form of paid advertising on the web these days is Google AdWords.

Google will allow you to pay to place ads around the Internet to drive traffic to your website. The cost of getting your ad to appear varies based on other advertisers looking to advertise in the same spot at the same time.

For example, if you want your advertisement to appear on a webpage that talks about how to make short sales in Baltimore (remember the example above where you were trying to get distressed seller leads in Baltimore), you will be competing with others who are interested in advertising space on the same page. These are either other investors like you who are trying to attract seller leads or real estate agents who are looking for clients. If you are willing to pay more than they are for the advertising space, Google will give it to you; if your competitors are willing to pay more, they will likely get it.

In addition to Google AdWords, savvy Internet Marketers will try to convince owners of valuable websites to dedicate advertising space for a fee. Using the example above, you might approach the Baltimore short sale webpage owner with an offer to pay a monthly fee to provide your advertisement with a permanent spot on their site. In general, using this type of paid advertising, you'll pay the site owner every time a page is displayed with your ad on it, regardless of whether your ad is clicked.

There are many intricacies of Internet Marketing, but if you have an aptitude for working online and the time and energy to become an expert Internet Marketer, this is another excellent way to potentially find investment leads from your target sellers.

Other Marketing Techniques

To name just a few of the other potential ways to find deals:

- Newspaper/magazine classified ads
- Display ads in restaurants/bars
- Radio spots
- Television spots
- Billboards
- Social networking
- Partnering with professionals who deal with distressed sellers (agents, attorneys, etc.)

While many of the techniques popular among investors to generate leads and deals are covered, this is certainly meant to be a partial list. There are hundreds, if not thousands, of ways to market for potential sales; these are just some.

Keys to Great Direct Mail Marketing Campaigns

Creating successful direct marketing campaigns will take a lot of time and practice. Most likely, the first set of letters or postcards you send won't receive the response you were anticipating; this is why good direct marketers will spend lots of time honing and testing every aspect of their campaigns to get the highest response rate.

If you want to be a great direct marketer and have effective direct mail campaigns, you must be willing to test many different approaches and be glad to keep going despite adversity or low response rates. Here are just a few things that good direct marketers do in the course of creating and optimizing a D.M. campaign:

- Test different-sized letters or postcards
- Test different-sized envelopes
- Test handwritten vs. typed letters and envelopes
- Test different color papers and inks
- Test different kinds of stamps (first class vs. bulk)
- Test different marketing messages
- Test different target groups (distressed vs. retail, homeowner vs. investor, etc.)

There are thousands of different permutations for how you can put together your marketing campaign. There is no one right way to be successful with direct mail -- you need to figure out what works for your target sellers in your area and your market. Remember, what works for one group of potential sellers at one particular time and in one specific market may not work for another group of potential sellers at another time and in another market.

As an example, use a handwritten yellow letter absentee owner mail campaign:

Dear [First Name],

Hi,

My Name is J

I would like to BUY your house at

[Address]

Please call me at

[Phone]

Thanks, J

With that being said, there are four key elements crucial to achieving success as a direct marketer:

1. Captivating your audience's attention.

When sending out letters, it is essential to engage the recipient's interest and motivate them to open the envelope and explore its contents. One effective strategy is to personalize the envelope, giving it the appearance of an invitation rather than a formal business letter. Utilize greeting card-sized envelopes, handwrite the address, exclude your business name from the return address label, and consider using pastel-colored envelopes. These techniques will help pique curiosity.

2. Ensuring your message is consumed.

It is vital that your message is not only read but also establishes an emotional connection with the prospect. This connection should prompt them to take action, such as calling you or visiting your website for further information. To achieve this, personalize your message and consider using a handwritten font or mail merge to simulate a handwritten appearance. By incorporating the prospect's name and address into the message, you increase the likelihood of it being read and generating an emotional response. Importantly, this approach creates a personalized feel while still relying on automated processes.

3. Inspiring your audience to act upon your call to action.

Your objective is to motivate the recipient to pick up the phone, browse your website, send an email, or perform any other action you desire. The most effective approach is to tailor your message in a way that convinces the recipient that you possess the solution to their problems. People are more likely to respond when they believe that taking action will alleviate their concerns.

4. Converting potential leads into successful sales.

Converting a prospect into a customer requires more than a single interaction; it often takes days or even weeks of consistent effort. Your responsibility is to persuade the seller that you have the ability to solve their problems and instill confidence in your capabilities. Conquering this step is undoubtedly the most challenging aspect of being a successful marketer. If you find it difficult to communicate effectively with potential leads or prefer not to engage in direct communication, consider enlisting the help of someone who can. Even if you can attract 100% of your target audience to reach out, it is essential to possess the skills necessary to convert those leads into profitable transactions.

The Secret to Direct Mail Marketing Success

There is one HUGE secret that successful direct marketers do that other, less successful, direct marketers need to do. And that is repetition.

Too many new marketers assume that if they don't get a response from a prospect on the first mailing, they'll never get a response. Nothing could be further from the truth. You're more likely to get an answer (even if it's just a "TAKE ME OFF YOUR LIST!!!") on the second, third, fourth, or fifth mailing than on the first. Even if the Prospect is only calling to ask to be removed from the list, that's still an opportunity to try to convert a lead.

If you want to be successful with direct mail marketing, communicate consistently. Send a second mailing 2-3 weeks after the first, a third mailing 4-6 weeks after that, and then follow up with additional mailings every 6-8 weeks for the next several months.

Letter Sample 1:

Dear [Prospect],

My name is [Name]. I'm reaching out as a investor, and I wanted to extend a warm welcome to the [Location] neighborhood. I hope you're enjoying the area.

Navigating the real estate market can be overwhelming, especially when you're handling everything on your own. If you ever have any questions or need guidance, don't hesitate to reach out. I'm here to help.

Whether you're looking to buy a new home or considering selling, I'm just a phone call away, ready to provide you with all the answers and support you need. Feel free to contact me anytime.

Best regards,

[Your Name]

Letter Sample 2:

Dear [Client name],

I hope this letter finds you in good health and high spirits. I know that you have been at your home for [insert time period] at [Address]. I wanted to check in and see how everything is going.

You may not be aware, but home prices in your area have reached record highs lately, with many properties selling for as much as $[maximum sales estimate]. With limited inventory, eager buyers are willing to pay top dollar for homes like yours. Therefore, I wanted to bring this opportunity to your attention.

Several potential buyers have expressed interest in homes within [City or Neighborhood]. If you're open to exploring the possibility of selling, I would be delighted to discuss it further. Please feel free to contact me at your convenience.

Warm regards,

[Your Name]

Neighborhood sales:

Hello [Sellers Name],

I'm [Your Name]. I have been assisting homeowners with their property transactions in [neighborhood] for [period] years. Most recently, I have assisted your neighbor with their home and would like to assist you as well.

If you are considering selling your property, I would be thrilled to offer my assistance. The current market shows a significant interest in homes within your neighborhood, making it an opportune time to take advantage of the increased demand for properties like yours.

Whether you are planning to sell soon or simply want to explore your options, please don't hesitate to get in touch for a no-obligation price evaluation. I'm here to provide you with the information and guidance you need.

Sincerely,

[Your Name]

As you become more comfortable finding what best works for you, marketing will be more cost-effective and produce quality leads. Remember, this will take some time and some heavy lifting upfront. Once you determine the best methods of lead generation, you will start to build a solid lead list.

Thus far, we have looked at all relevant information for you to acquire a home. Whether you're purchasing a home for an investment or for personal use, these methods can be applied to both. The last piece of the puzzle is financing. There has been mention of what you can do with financing. Now, let's discuss the financing types used in a real estate transaction.

MODULE 5: **FINANCE**

5.1 Why You Need to Understand Real Estate Financing

This section attempts to provide you with a thorough overview of the many forms of real estate financing accessible for your real estate transactions. We looked at many investment vehicles in earlier modules, including single-family houses, commercial real estate, apartments, and more. We also reviewed several real estate profit techniques such as buy and hold, flipping, and wholesaling.

While not complete, the list below will provide you with a solid understanding of various financing techniques used by real estate investors. By obtaining a wide grasp of these strategies, you may efficiently manage any real estate investment by combining an investment vehicle, an investment strategy, and a financing methodology.

5.2 All Cash

Some investors opt to fully finance their investment properties using their own funds. According to a research conducted by BiggerPockets and Memphis Invest, 24% of investors in the United States choose to utilize 100% of their personal finances to support their real estate ventures. However, it's important to note that the term "All Cash" commonly used in these transactions doesn't involve physical currency. Instead, the buyer typically provides a certified money check, such as a bank cashier's check, to the title company, or the funds are electronically transferred through wire transfer. Although this approach represents the most straightforward form of funding, it may not be feasible for many investors, especially those who are just starting out. Moreover, the returns from an all-cash transaction differ from those achieved through leveraging. Let's explore the following example to illustrate this point:

For instance, consider John, who possesses $100,000 available for investment. He can choose to employ this capital to purchase a property that generates a monthly income of $1,000, resulting in an annual return of $12,000, equivalent to a 12% return on investment. On the other hand, John could allocate the $100,000 as a 20% down payment on five comparable residences, each valued at $100,000. By securing an $80,000 mortgage on each property, the rental income from each home would amount to approximately $300 per month, totaling $1,500 per month or $18,000 per year. This translates to an 18% return on investment, which is 50% higher than acquiring a single property.

5.3 Conventional Mortgage

As demonstrated in the previous example, financing an investment property through traditional methods can lead to higher returns compared to an all-cash purchase. Consequently, most investors opt to finance their assets using a down payment and a conventional mortgage. Conventional mortgages typically require a 20% down payment, although this percentage may vary from 25% to 30% for investment properties, depending on the lender. Among homebuyers, conventional mortgages are widely favored due to their lower interest rates.

5.4 Portfolio Lenders

Portfolio lenders, on the other hand, represent a category of lenders that directly provide loans using their own funds. While conventional mortgage loans are often sourced from banks, mortgage brokers, and credit unions, these lenders typically obtain financing from other parties or resell loans to government-backed entities like Fannie Mae and Freddie Mac. Consequently, these institutions must adhere to stringent regulations and restrictions when financing projects, which can pose challenges for real estate investors and self-employed borrowers seeking traditional financing.

However, certain banks and credit unions function as portfolio lenders, utilizing their own funds for lending purposes. This classification enables them to offer more flexible loan terms and qualification criteria based on their own standards. Portfolio lenders often have less rigid eligibility requirements compared to traditional lenders.

Although portfolio lenders may not explicitly advertise their services as such, they can be identified through recommendations and networking with other investors. Alternatively, reaching out to individual lenders and inquiring about their portfolio financing options is another approach.

5.5 FHA Loans

Another financing option is FHA loans, which are provided by the Federal Housing Administration, a federal organization in the United States that insures bank mortgages. These loans are primarily intended for homeowners who wish to reside in the property and are not suitable for pure investment properties. However, there is an exception that allows FHA-financed properties to include up to four separate units, such as duplexes, triplexes, or four-plexes, wherein the borrower can reside in one of the units.

One notable advantage of an FHA loan is the low down payment requirement, currently set at 3.5%. This can be advantageous for individuals looking to embark on their real estate journey sooner without having to accumulate the conventional 20% down payment. However, there is an additional cost known as Private Mortgage Insurance (PMI) associated with FHA loans when the down payment is less than 20%. PMI protects the lender and may slightly increase the monthly payment while reducing cash flow.

5.6 203K Loans

203K loans are a specific type of FHA loan designed for homeowners who want to purchase a property that requires rehabilitation. These loans allow borrowers to include the cost of necessary repairs or renovations in the loan amount. Similar to conventional FHA loans, 203K loans have a low down payment requirement of only 3.5%. They can be used for duplexes, triplexes, and fourplexes, but they are only available for owner-occupied homes. Additionally, Private Mortgage Insurance is required for loans with a down payment of less than 20%.

Let's consider a real-world example to illustrate the concept. John comes across a modest duplex priced at $100,000 and intends to live in one half while renting out the other. The property requires approximately $12,000 for fresh paint and flooring. By incorporating this $12,000 into the loan amount, John can make a 3.5% down payment of $3,920 on the total loan. With the loan covering the renovation costs, John can move into his remodeled property, rent out the other unit, and start generating cash flow and building wealth. This arrangement suits John's goals well.

5.7 HomePath Mortgages

Another government-backed lending program established by Fannie Mae, called HomePath Mortgage, aims to revitalize non-performing loans (properties that have been fore-closed on) and convert them into viable loans once again. HomePath loans, similar to FHA loans, feature lower down payment requirements (now as low as 10%), but unlike FHA loans, they do not require mortgage insurance. This lending option is available to investors and properties that are not owner-occupied. Like the 203K FHA loan discussed earlier, HomePath allows for financing renovations as part of the purchase. It's important to note that these loans are only available for Fannie Mae-owned bank-owned homes. To find eligible properties, you can visit the HomePath website at HomePath.com.

5.8 Owner Financing

Owner financing is an alternative to traditional property financing that doesn't involve banks or major lending organizations. In some cases, the property owner may provide the financing, and the buyer makes monthly payments directly to the owner instead of a bank. This option is typically chosen by property owners who own the property free and clear, meaning they don't have an existing mortgage. If the seller has another outstanding debt and decides to sell the property, the loan must be paid off immediately to avoid foreclosure. This is due to a legal provision known as the "Due on Sale" clause, which gives the previous lender the right to demand immediate payment. Failure to pay could lead to foreclosure. Some investors choose to bypass this condition and acquire the property "subject to" the existing loan, assuming that the bank will not foreclose.

Owner financing can be a viable option for purchasing real estate without involving a bank, but the requirements and risks should be carefully considered. It may also be beneficial in the future when selling the property.

5.9 Hard Money

"Hard money" refers to financing obtained from private firms or individuals for the purpose of investing in real estate. Hard money loans have several distinctive features:

- The loan is primarily based on the value of the property.
- Shorter loan terms (typically 6 to 36 months).
- Higher interest rates (ranging from 8% to 15%).
- Costly loan "points" (fees associated with obtaining the loan).
- Many hard money lenders do not require income verification or credit references.
- Hard money loans do not appear on your credit report.
- Hard money lenders are familiar with properties that need rehabilitation work and can often finance a transaction within a few days.

When seeking hard money loans, it is important to exercise caution and fully understand the risks involved. While hard money can be useful for short-term loans and certain situations, some investors have faced difficulties after the loan period ended. To mitigate potential issues, it is crucial to have multiple exit options in place before obtaining a hard money loan.

If you are looking for a hard money lender, here are some tips to help you choose a reputable option:

- Consult a real estate agent who has experience with real estate investing.
- Seek advice from a house flipper who has utilized hard money loans in the past.
- An internet search can provide a list or resources, but do you due diligence.

5.10 Private Money

Private money, on the other hand, is similar to hard money but differs in the lender-borrower relationship. Private money lenders are often individuals seeking higher returns on their money rather than professional lenders. Private money loans may require a pre-existing personal connection with the lender, who is typically less business-oriented. Additionally, private money loans often have lower fees and points, and the loan terms can be more flexible to accommodate both parties.

When borrowing from a private lender, they provide you with funds to purchase a property in exchange for a specific interest rate. The lender's investment is secured by a promissory note or mortgage on the property, allowing them to foreclose and take ownership of the property in the event of nonpayment, similar to banks, hard money lenders, or other loan types. Private money loans typically have a fixed interest rate and a predetermined loan duration, ranging from six months to thirty years.

In most cases, private lenders do not receive an ownership stake in the property's future cash flow or value beyond the agreed-upon interest rate. However, the terms of private financing can vary, and agreements may differ. Private money loans are commonly used when there is an expectation of increasing the property's value within a short period. Once the value has increased, you can assume the debt from the private money loan, refinance the property, and repay the private lender. Similar to hard money loans, private money should only be pursued when you have well-defined exit strategies in place.

Building trust and cultivating relationships for private funding is crucial. You can achieve this by actively promoting your real estate ventures through channels such as blogging about your experiences, sharing updates on social media platforms like Facebook, engaging in casual conversations about real estate investing, or participating in local real estate investment clubs. Increasing your exposure and providing opportunities to share your investing experience is important. While you don't need to boast, take advantage of chances to share information about your real estate ventures when someone shows interest. You never know what positive outcomes may arise from these relationships.

5.11 Home Equity Loans and Lines of Credit

When considering the acquisition of investment properties, many investors opt to utilize the equity in their home property as a funding source. Banks and other lenders offer various products, such as Home Value Installment Loans (HEIL) or Home Equity Lines of Credit (HELOC), which allow borrowers to borrow against the value of their homes. For instance, instead of directly financing the investment property, an investor may choose to take out a HELOC on their house to cover the property's cost.

To qualify for a home equity loan or line of credit, it is necessary to have equity in your house. Lenders typically set a maximum loan amount based on a percentage of the home's value. While this percentage varies among lenders, it is common to find banks willing to lend up to 90% of the home's worth.

Let's illustrate how this works with an example: John owns a house valued at $100,000, and his bank allows him to borrow up to 90% of the property's value. This means that John can borrow up to $90,000 from the equity in his home. If he already has a $50,000 first mortgage, the home equity line or loan would be limited to $40,000 to ensure that the total debt does not exceed 90% of the home's value.

Utilizing home equity loans and lines of credit instead of regular loans offers several benefits, including:

- The loan is based on the valuation of your primary residence rather than the recently purchased property. This means that the lender is primarily concerned with the new property and not with how you plan to use the funds or the condition of the property.
- With a home equity loan or line of credit, you have the flexibility to spend the money as you see fit. It is not tied to the new property, allowing you to make "cash" bids on new properties and increase your chances of acceptance.
- Home equity loans and lines of credit may offer special tax advantages, such as the ability to deduct the interest paid on the loan, as permitted by the IRS. For more information, it is advisable to consult with a certified CPA or attorney.
- Since your primary residence serves as collateral, interest rates for home equity loans and lines are often lower compared to hard money or private money loans.

Another common approach employed by investors is using a portion of their home equity to cover the down payment on an investment property. For instance, let's consider Sarah, an investor who wants to purchase a $100,000 investment property but lacks sufficient funds for a down payment. However, Sarah has significant potential equity in her primary residence, owing $50,000 on a $100,000 home. In this case, Sarah can obtain a conventional mortgage from a bank for the remaining $80,000 needed for the investment property and open a $20,000 home equity loan on her house to fulfill the down payment requirement.

When contemplating home equity loans and lines of credit, it is crucial to compare fixed and adjustable interest rates and align them with your investment objectives, timelines, and financial situation.

5.12 Partnerships

When considering investing in a property that surpasses your financial means, partnering with an equity investor can be a valuable addition to your team. An equity partner is someone you bring onboard to assist with financing the property. Equity partnerships can be structured in various ways, such as utilizing the partner's capital to fully finance the property or having them contribute to the down payment. While there are no strict guidelines for equity partnerships, each situation requires careful analysis of how value will be generated, decision-making authority, and profit sharing.

The level of involvement of the equity partner in the property is determined by a mutually agreed-upon operating agreement. Due to their ownership position, equity partners have the opportunity to actively participate in various aspects of property ownership. Moreover, as partners, they typically earn a return on their investment based on their ownership stake, which encompasses cash flow, appreciation, depreciation, and eventual profit upon the property's sale.

Unlike private lenders, equity partners do not receive a fixed interest rate on their investments. Instead, their returns are directly tied to a proportion of the property's generated revenue. If the property yields substantial earnings, their return will be more significant. Conversely, if the investment incurs losses, they may need to contribute additional funds to sustain the property. Compared to private lenders, equity partners assume greater risks, but they also have the potential for higher rewards if the investment proves successful. Additionally, unlike private financing, the equity partner's investment is secured by an operational agreement rather than a mortgage or promissory note.

5.13 Commercial Loans

When considering investments in properties beyond one to four-unit residential buildings, commercial financing provides a potential avenue for funding. If you're looking to purchase a property that doesn't fall under the residential category, a business loan is the appropriate choice.

Compared to residential loans, commercial loans typically have slightly higher interest rates, fees, shorter terms, and different qualification requirements. While residential lending primarily considers the borrower's income, commercial financing places greater emphasis on the property itself. The underlying rationale is straightforward: if you own a ten-million-dollar apartment complex and encounter financial difficulties, you must meet the mortgage payments regardless of whether your personal income is $20,000 or $200,000 per year. Commercial lenders assess factors such as your income, creditworthiness, and other specific financial indicators, but their primary focus lies in evaluating your financial capabilities. In most cases, the revenue-generating potential of the property carries more significance.

Furthermore, commercial lenders often offer a "business line of credit" that can be utilized to finance property flips and other real estate ventures. Certain investors may qualify for a substantial business line of credit, enabling them to access capital for activities like home flipping and other real estate projects.

YOUR NEXT STEPS

We've covered all the essential elements of investing in real estate and home ownership. Now comes the exciting part – putting what you've learned into action! Take some time to go through each module independently. By doing so, you'll be equipped to handle your real estate investment journey with confidence. Here is a quick synopsis of each module:

Module 1 – Mindset: In order to create generational wealth, you need to have a positive mindset. Take into consideration that this may be the most difficult part of the process. It makes you relearn things you thought you knew, and that's OK.

Module 2 – What do you want your money to do for you? Determine what you want to do with your money and what it's supposed to do for you, and then plan for it.

Module 3 – Types of Real Estate Investments: There are many options for investing in real estate. Once you've done your research, identify what type of real estate you're comfortable investing in.

Module 4 – Resources: Your contract is the final say on how the deal will be constructed. Some tools have been given for your review and understanding. There may be additional resources that you find that you can add to what you have thus far.

Module 5 – Finance: Ensure that you determine how you are going to financially support your investment and what financial structure works for you over time.

Read each module again in its entirety, and then execute. You will have questions and doubts, and that's OK. The only thing left to do is put a plan together and be action-oriented. Remember, you will need to be in the right mindset to succeed, but succeed, you will. Things to keep in mind: do your due diligence, create a power team, ask questions, and create a plan. Go to real estate seminars. Join groups, speak with real estate agents, and find a mentor. Read additional books. Whatever it is that you do, educate yourself on what it takes to become an avid real estate investor. The goal is to build wealth, generational wealth. Wealth that has been created by you but has allowed the future generation to be financially secure.

You are on the correct path of wealth generation. Congratulations!

ABOUT THE AUTHOR

Anthony C. Bailey is a highly accomplished professional with a remarkable career spanning over two decades in the real estate industry. Throughout his journey, he has held key leadership positions, earning a reputation for championing business process success and cultivating on-site change management objectives. With a diverse skill set, strategic acumen, and a relentless drive for excellence, Anthony has inspired trust among peers and stakeholders alike.

Anthony served as Deputy Director, where he honed his expertise in optimizing operational systems and driving business process improvements. With a keen eye for quality control and resource management, Anthony played a pivotal role in streamlining daily operations and developing robust organizational planning strategies. As the primary point of contact for legal matters, he exhibited strong problem-solving skills and a comprehensive understanding of governing instruments.

As the Managing Director of Lumarjo Holdings LLC, Anthony showcased his entrepreneurial prowess by strategically investing in technology, real estate, and brand development initiatives led by people of color. Implementing an aggressive strategic growth plan, he ensured that all investments contributed to the company's return on investment (ROI). His collaborative approach with cross-functional teams exemplified his dedication to consistent business growth and goal achievement.

During his tenure as a Business Analyst, Anthony excelled in conducting market analyses and driving improvements in

IT systems across the organization. He skillfully managed off-shore technology consultants for POS systems and demonstrated exceptional communication skills when interacting with business stakeholders. With a focus on cost control measures and strategic solutions, Anthony contributed significantly to the business's profitability.

As the Information Technology Director at a media organization, Anthony showcased his versatility by managing the company's technology operations and implementing new IT systems and policies. He was instrumental in creating and managing an IP television platform and executing effective marketing strategies that led to a 45% increase in listenership. Anthony's continuous focus on creative outreach initiatives played a vital role in entertaining and informing the business market.

In addition to his professional achievements, Anthony's commitment to academic excellence is evident in his pursuit of a Ph.D. in Business Administration with a focus on Business from Hampton University. He also holds a Master's in Business Administration and a Bachelor's in Music with a concentration in Production, reflecting his passion for continuous learning and growth.

Anthony's involvement in various community organizations further underscores his dedication to making a positive impact. As a Board Member he has actively contributed to social causes. Additionally, his role as the First Vice President of the PTA highlights his commitment to education and community development.

Beyond his professional pursuits, Anthony's creativity shines through in his involvement as an Executive Producer for the festivals and a Brand Developer and Co-Creator for a co-working space. These endeavors showcase his ability to think outside the box and create unique experiences.

With a wealth of experience, a passion for real estate, and a proven track record of driving change, Anthony C. Bailey is the perfect candidate to author a how-to-book about real estate. Readers can trust in his insights and expertise, knowing that he possesses the knowledge and vision to guide them through the complexities of the real estate world. As a visionary real estate expert and change management specialist, Anthony C. Bailey's book promises to empower readers and equip them with the tools they need to succeed in their own real estate ventures.

www.AnthonyCBailey.com

Made in the USA
Middletown, DE
05 October 2024

61718719R00077